COLD COMFORT

SCOTT MACKAY

CARROLL & GRAF PUBLISHERS, INC.
NEW YORK

First Carroll & Graf edition 1998

Carroll & Graf Publishers, Inc.
19 West 21st Street
New York, NY 10010

Library of Congress Cataloging-in-Publication Data is available

ISBN: 0-7867-0507-8

Manufactured in the United States of America

To my father, Jack

Acknowledgments

I would like to gratefully acknowledge Staff Inspector
Ken Cenzura and Detective Mark Mendelson of the
Metropolitan Toronto Police Force Homicide Squad for their
kindly given advice, information, and time.

I would also like to thank Lawrence Nabozniak for his su-
perb information on firearms ballistics; Ken Doggett for his
thoughts and information on government tendering processes;
Kent Carroll and Adam Dunn for their excellent editorial support; Joshua Bilmes, my agent; and Janet Hutchings, of *Ellery
Queen's Mystery Magazine*.

Finally, thanks to J. D. Singh, of The Sleuth of Baker Street
Book Store.

Author's Note

Though most of the places and institutions in this book have real-life counterparts, the characters and events are solely the products of the author's imagination. The author has the highest regard for the Metropolitan Toronto Police Force, its Homicide Squad, and its detectives. His fictional counterparts, though based on real life, are still imaginary, and shouldn't be construed to represent actual real-life organizations or persons.

COLD
COMFORT

Chapter One

Detective Barry Gilbert stood with his hands in his pockets, his collar up to protect his neck from the frigid north wind, and stared at the body. A young woman, around thirty, lying face down, knees partially bent, her blonde hair blowing across her left cheek. February 18, the coldest day so far, with a windchill of minus 40 Celsius, and the woman was frozen solid, no telling when she died, no wallet, no purse, no coat or hat, wearing a baggy sweatshirt, black exercise tights, and running shoes. He looked up. He knew the uniforms wanted to get back into their patrol cars. He gazed across the icy expanse of the harbor where he saw the city—the sleek bank buildings, the Skydome, the C.N. Tower. The harbor was ice-bound. Most of Lake Ontario was ice-bound. There hadn't been a winter this cold in a long time.

He took a few steps back then went around to the other side of the corpse. He looked up the pier road to Cherry Street. Where was that detective from Auto Squad? The pier road was blown bare by the wind, but tongue-like drifts of snow with tire tracks through them extended here and there from the ditches. Tony Malcolm from the Forensic Identification Unit photographed the tracks.

Gilbert squatted. He looked at the woman's left hand; a ragged gash about two inches long gaped from the fleshy side of her palm. Frozen open. How did she get that gash? It certainly wasn't a defense wound. A bite mark? Cause of death wasn't readily apparent. The young woman had been dumped here after the fact, on the edge of the pier, next to the looming silos of the Dominion Malting Company.

His partner, Detective Joe Lombardo, walked across the gravel parking lot from the adjoining offices of Dominion Malting. He hopped over the shallow ditch and came to the edge of the pier.

"He's inside," said Lombardo. "Whenever you're ready."

"Where's Auto Squad?" asked Gilbert.

Lombardo shrugged. "Are we going to roll her?" he asked.

"Not yet." Gilbert pointed to the barley silos. "I want to go up there. I want to see what things look like from up there."

They both looked at the nearest silo; a zigzagging fire escape went to the top.

"Are you sure it's safe?" asked Lombardo.

Gilbert stared at the fire escape. "I'll take my chances," he said.

He walked across the parking lot to the silo. His eyes strayed over the ground. The ground here was bare, landfill, added inch by inch over the years to what used to be marshland. He stooped.

Barley kernel studded the ground. He glanced back toward the body. Kernels were frozen into the ground everywhere. Also, the ground was darker. Like it had old coal mixed in with it.

"Hey, Tony, I want you to take some of this dirt back," he called.

Tony nodded.

At the foot of the metal stairs he again looked back at the body and calculated a rough distance. Always taking distances, as if death were something that could be measured. He began the climb. Lately he felt tired, and he was having a hard time remembering which murder was which. The wind whistled through the steel slats of the steps. His footsteps clanked dully. This one might stand out. Frozen solid. A young woman, as yet unidentified. He felt sorry for her, whoever she was; she looked like a real victim. And she looked so alone on the edge of the pier like that, so cold and abandoned, with the snow drifting against her body. Crazy thought, but he somehow wanted to comfort her, maybe because she reminded him, with her blonde hair, of his daughter, Jennifer. He wanted to take his coat off and drape it over her frozen form.

When he reached the top of the silo, he clutched his collar tightly to his throat. The wind needled him with polar intensity. The sun, a taut white ball, shone far to the south. The L-shaped archipelago of the Toronto Islands sliced the inner harbor. Lake Ontario was an infinite windswept expanse of white. The coldest day of the year. Gilbert wondered if there was any significance to that, if the weather had played a part in this murder. He looked down at the crime scene. Two patrol cars, their own forest green Lumina, and Tony Malcolm's van were parked a good distance from the body. He looked at the pattern the tire tracks made through the intermittent drifts of snow. Over the wind, he heard the hum of the morning rush hour on the Gardiner Expressway. He concentrated on the tire tracks nearest the body, traced them through the intermittent drifts of snow to Cherry Street. Most tracks turned left, back toward town. One set, however, turned right, past the Knob Hill Food Terminal. Toward Cherry Beach.

He and Lombardo got in the Lumina and drove toward Cherry Beach while the uniforms waited for the Auto Squad man to come.

"How's that girl working out?" asked Lombardo.

Gilbert pushed the heater right to the top, but it didn't make much difference; they were both freezing.

"Which girl?"

"The one that's staying at your house. The exchange student. The one from Denmark."

The area around Cherry Beach was desolate; boarded up warehouses lined the street, abandoned equipment dotted vacant fields, and condemned lakers, their hulls rusted out and their windows smashed, floated frozen in the ice.

"She's not from Denmark," said Gilbert. "She's from Germany."

"Yeah, her. What's her name?"

"Joe, if you have any ideas . . . she's going to be gone the first week of March. And as far as I know she's got a boyfriend back in Frankfurt. She's way too young for you. She's only nineteen."

"Who said anything about having ideas? I just wanted to know her name."

"Valerie."

"Valerie," said Joe, testing the name in his mouth. A frown came to his face. "That doesn't sound German to me. What's a girl from Germany doing with a name like that?"

Gilbert ignored the question, leaned forward, looked for the tracks in the intermittent snowdrifts. "I don't see them," he said. "I think we lost them."

Lombardo shifted forward and peered out the windshield. "They're over there," he said, pointing to the beach road turn-off. "You see them?"

Gilbert nodded and turned left. "Let's see what we've got."

The car bounced over the dirt road. Tall poplars lined either side of the narrow single-track road. The track dead-ended at a small parking area at the beach. The lake was no more than twenty-five meters away, flat, bleak, with snow ghosts prancing everywhere in the wind. Gilbert stopped the car at the entrance to the parking lot. They both could immediately see that there was only one set of tire tracks in there. He looked at the volleyball net, the swings, the teeter-totters; these were the things of summer, yet now they were frozen in deepest winter.

They got out of the car and walked over to the far side of the parking lot, careful not to disturb any of the tracks. The tracks stopped abruptly at the edge.

"This is where he parked," said Gilbert.

They looked at the impressions in the snow: footprints, one on top of the other, especially around the trunk, all made by the same pair of boots.

"Looks like he dropped her here," said Lombardo, pointing. "That's a head and that's an arm."

The two detectives crouched. The impression in the snow reminded Gilbert of a modern sculpture, like one of the Henry Moore's at the art gallery, with the figure's component parts reduced to the bare minimums: the head was now no more than a ball, the torso a tapering wedge, and the hip an oval.

"So our suspect's a man," said Lombardo.

Gilbert glanced over at the footprints; men's boots, snow boots, with a deep tread. "I would say so."

"And he dropped her here at the back of the car."

"Yep."

"But she didn't struggle. There's no marks, nothing that indicates movement. She was already dead when he dropped her here."

Gilbert stood up and looked at the pattern the tire tracks made. He parked here, he dumped her here, then for one reason or another he put her back in the trunk, drove her to the pier and dumped her there. Why? He scanned the scene. Immediately before them, the snow had been swept bare from the frozen sand. But where it started again he now saw footprints leading down to the edge of the beach. He pointed.

"Let's go check this."

They walked toward the beach. They followed the footprints all the way to the lake; the wind was much stronger here and the prints weren't as good. At the end, another body impression, this one a bit different, the hips flaring much wider.

"She was on her back here," said Gilbert.

"Is that blood?" asked Lombardo.

The detectives again crouched. Rust-red patches blotched the snow, not much, hardly the copious amounts of blood one would expect from a fatal knife or bullet wound.

"You think he killed her here?" asked Lombardo.

Gilbert stood up and gazed out at the lake, his eyes squinting against the snowy brightness. What a place to die. The way the wind teased the snow out on the ice shelf reminded him of desert sand; the snow was piled into drifts and sculpted into ridges, like a scene from the Sahara, only everything was white.

"We've got to get that blood," he said. "We'll send Tony down."

Back at the pier, the Auto Squad Detective still hadn't arrived. The uniforms had coffee now. One of them was just finishing up with the yellow crime-scene tape.

"Benny Pompa's probably getting tired of waiting," said Lombardo.

"I want to roll her now," said Gilbert. "Let's get a good look at her."

Gilbert crouched by the body, memorizing all the details, wondering if there were something he had missed, something that wouldn't show up in the photographs. She was well-groomed. She wasn't wearing a wedding ring, but there was definitely a groove around her ring finger; maybe it was a simple robbery. Or maybe sexual assault. Her hair was cut short, jaw length, looked well-washed, and her clothes were clean, expensive, fairly new. She wasn't a street person. She wasn't living on the fringe. This was a victim from the main-stream. This woman looked as if she had a job.

"Wait a minute," said Gilbert, pointing. "Look at this."

Lombardo crouched next to her. Hidden among the folds of her mauve sweatshirt lay several long brown hairs, caught on the fabric. The hairs were fine; they looked like hair from a woman's head, but definitely not the blonde hairs from the victim's head. Lombardo pulled an evidence envelope and tweezers from his pocket, bagged the hairs, and made a no-tation on the label.

"Can we roll her now?" asked Lombardo. "I'm freezing."

Gilbert shrugged. "Might as well."

The two men gently gripped the body and turned it over. The arms and legs remained stiff, frozen into position by the extreme cold, but the waist gave a little. They immediately saw the gunshot wound to her chest.

"No exit wound," said Gilbert. "Maybe the bullet's still in there."

"Have you ever seen a gunshot wound like that?" said Lombardo. "Her shirt should be soaked in blood."

Gilbert took the woman's shirt and gently pulled it up. She wasn't wearing a bra; her breasts were small and looked strange because they were frozen into place, stood upright, defying gravity. The wound itself was nothing more than a small blood-free hole. Both men were puzzled.

"I guess this is one for Blackstein," said Gilbert.

He took one last look at the woman's face. Somehow the face seemed familiar. She had a gentle face, pretty, innocent, pixieish. Some frost had accumulated on her cheeks. But underneath the frost Gilbert saw some freckles. He shook his head. Against his better judgment, he rubbed away some of the frost.

"Let's go talk to Pompa," he said.

Benny Pompa, a security guard with Dominion Malting for twenty-two years, a short rotund man who spoke with a heavy Italian accent, sat at his desk in the reception area. When the detectives entered, he looked up with glum apprehension. He was around fifty years old. The other employees were streaming in, casting nervous glances at Benny and the detectives.

"We won't take much of your time, Mr. Pompa," said Gilbert. "We just want to get your statement."

Pompa said something in Italian to Joe; Joe responded then turned to Gilbert. "He says we're making all the ladies nervous."

Gilbert nodded. "Mr. Pompa, could you tell me what time you discovered the body?"

Pompa told them, in his accented English, how every morning he drove to the end of Cherry Street to gaze out at the lake while he had his first cigarette.

"Very cold this morning," he said. "And dark. You couldn't see a thing. I finish my cigarette and I drive back here. I start at six-thirty. I drive to the parking lot—I park in the same spot every day, down near the *Charles Lougheed*—

my headlights swing by the pier, still very dark, and I see what I think is a bag of garbage, sometimes you get that, people coming down here to dump, the city won't take it so they decide they'll get rid of it themselves. I see any garbage, I'm supposed to take it to the Dumpster. We don't want more seagulls and rats than we already have."

"So this was around six-thirty?" said Gilbert.

"Around that."

"And you're always the first one here in the morning?"

"Always."

"So you drove down to the end of Cherry Street," said Gilbert. "I gather you didn't see any other cars."

"No," said Pompa. "I was the only one down there."

"And you saw no suspicious activity at all?"

"No."

"Could you see the beach?"

"Through the trees, yes, I could."

"Were there any cars in the parking area?" asked Gilbert.

"No."

"So you saw what you thought was a bag of garbage by the *Charles Lougheed*. Then what did you do?"

Pompa scratched behind his ear, where Gilbert saw a mole the size of a raisin. "I went to get it. The Dumpster's out behind here. I figure why make two trips when it's so cold. I'll put it in the Dumpster while I'm still outside. I'll use my head. So I walked over and I was about halfway there when I realized it wasn't a garbage bag. It was that poor lady. She's not moving. So I walk right up to her. I say to her, lady? Lady, are you all right? But she doesn't answer me. I see she doesn't have a coat on. I touch her with my toe. Nudge her."

Gilbert nodded. "Where did you nudge her?"

"I nudged her foot. And that's when I saw she was dead. So I came in here and called you guys."

*   *   *

The detective from the Auto Squad arrived five minutes later. He was a large man, in a ski jacket, about sixty years old, close to retirement, with stooped shoulders, a large nose, and watery blue eyes. His name was Laird, and he carried himself with a brusque efficiency few men mustered at his age. He glanced at the body then crouched by the nearest tire track. The wind brought two angry red spots to his face, while his nose was already webbed with a tracery of crimson varicose veins. His hands, ungloved, looked permanently stained with car grease.

He turned his head one way, then another, then took out a small pocket tape and measured the width of the track.

"That would be a Michelin XGT," he said, without preamble. He spoke with the remnants of a Scottish brogue. "Has to come from a big car, a luxury sedan. We see that particular Michelin on the Lincoln Town Car, the Crown Victoria, the Mercury Grand Marquis, the Buick Roadmaster . . ." He shook his head. "You see it on a lot of the larger luxury cars, about a dozen in all." He stood up and looked at the contralateral track. He measured the distance between the tracks. He slid his tape measure back into his pocket, took out a pack of Players Light, stuck one in his mouth, and lit up with a bulky brass lighter. He took a large pull and rubbed his nose with the back of his thumb, as if in this cold he had to make sure his nose was still there. "You give me the photos. I'll do some comparisons back at the shop. I might be able to narrow it down for you, but I doubt it. You've got a tough one here."

Gilbert and Lombardo watched the ambulance attendants slide the corpse onto the stretcher and cover it with an orange blanket. He would go home tonight to his wife and two daughters, and he would have a hot meal, and watch some television, and maybe browse through the latest issue of *National Geographic*. This woman would spend the night in the morgue. And once the girls were settled, and the furnace was humming in the basement, keeping them all warm, he and Regina would make love. And Regina's body would be soft, and her breasts would be pliant, and she would be breathing, and her heart would be pumping. She would be alive. This woman was dead. Even when they finally thawed her out she would still be cold. As he watched them load the woman's body into the back of the ambulance, he felt the old darkness coming back, his cynicism, and the sense that no matter how hard he tried he couldn't make a difference. This woman would never breathe again. And the blood would never move through her veins. He shook his head. There would never be any comfort for this woman ever again.

Chapter Two

Gilbert stood at the fourth-floor window of the duty room staring at Addison Cadillac and Buick across the street, listening to the detectives of the Homicide Squad gather behind him. He wasn't sure if he liked the new building here on College Street; he missed Jarvis Street. His eyes strayed to the corner, where cars, trucks, and buses rolled ceaselessly by on Bay Street. He missed the sense of community on Jarvis Street. He missed his coffee and brown toast at the Carlton Grill. He even missed the hookers on Isabella. Here on College Street, a few blocks from the Parliament Buildings, with the Coroner's Office just across the street, the sidewalks at lunch hour were thronged with civil servants. He missed all the old bag ladies with their bundle buggies, the panhandlers asking for change on Sherbourne Street, and the bright young kids from Jarvis Collegiate Institute.

He turned around. Lombardo approached with two cups of coffee. The young detective looked worried. His heavy brow had settled into an even line and his dark Piedmontese eyes smoldered with quiet wrath as he handed Gilbert his cup.

"I don't like it when Marsh calls a meeting out of the blue like this," said Lombardo.

Gilbert shrugged. "We've got to have meetings, Joe," he said.

"Why don't we have them in the office?"

"Because the office is too small."

Staff Inspector Bill Marsh, head of Homicide, entered the duty room carrying a few sheets of dog-eared paper. He was an older man, barrel-chested, with hair combed severely to the left, his face heavily wrinkled from years of liquid lunches. Today he wore meticulously creased grey flannels, black brogues, and a white dress shirt, sleeves rolled up, black tie loosened, tufts of grey chest hair spilling from the undone button at the top.

"Move in, move in," ordered Marsh. "I don't want to shout. Gilbert, Lombardo, get up here."

The two detectives moved forward. Gilbert looked around the room, caught Bob Bannatyne's eye, nodded, then scanned the rest of the room. The members of his team—Jim Groves, Petro Halycz, Gordon Telford—were staring at him, each of them looking to some extent as if they had been betrayed, as if they believed Gilbert had been holding back on them. Gilbert shrugged, trying to look puzzled.

"Are we all here?" asked Marsh. "Where's Birnbaum?"

"He's out on a case," said Hetherington.

"All right," said Marsh. He had a rough voice—too many years of smoking. "I'll tell him later." Marsh put his papers on the table; he looked out of place in this new modern building; he looked more at home in the dirt and clutter of the old one. "I'll give you the straight goods," he said. "Homicide has been asked to take a cut. We knew things were going to change once we moved up here. I'm sorry, but we don't have a choice. They look at our case clearance rate, and how it's dipped in the last few months, and they find their justifications. There's nothing I can do. Some of you are going to have to go."

Marsh stopped and looked at each and every one of the squad sergeants, Gilbert included; he perhaps looked at Gilbert longer than anyone.

"Ling calls me to his office, and he asks me, what's with these low clearance rates in Homicide? Why aren't you guys arresting anybody?"

Bob Bannatyne, one of the squad's veterans, spoke up. "You tell Ling, give us more manpower and we'll solve more murders. We haven't increased staff here in five years. But now we have more than double the murder rate. Tell him he can't read the numbers the old way anymore."

"You think I haven't told him that?" said Marsh. The Staff Inspector put his fists on his hips. "He says you got to work harder. They all think that way now. Ever since Tom Webb came down with his package last fall. Ling says to me, don't look at it as a cutback, look at it as a challenge. Don't look at it as more work, look at it as an opportunity."

Detective Fanshaw, from Kilbourn's quadrant, spoke up. "And meanwhile we haven't had a raise in five years. Meanwhile, they jack up the price of our long-term disability and completely discontinue our drug formulary so every time my little girl gets an ear infection I'm out twenty-five bucks for penicillin. And Ling says look at it as an opportunity?"

Marsh shrugged. "What do you want me to do?" he said. "I didn't vote Tory. I knew the Tories were going to do this from way back. You get a guy like Webb in there and you know the axe is going to fall."

Gilbert asked, "So how big a cut are we looking at?"

Marsh looked at him, then at all the other detectives.

"Eighteen percent over the next three years," he said. "And that's for everyone. Burglary, Vice, Sex Crimes, the SIU, the Bomb Squad, everybody. Some of you guys are going to be bumped, maybe back to patrol, maybe somewhere else. And I'm sorry, but some of you will just be canned outright, so you better start working on your resumes. Seven percent by April, six percent next year, and five percent the next. That's the way it is. That's what we got to deal with."

When Gilbert left the duty room and went back downstairs to the office, Carol Reid, one of the squad's secretaries, handed him a message slip: Dr. Blackstein. Please call.

He looked at Carol Reid as she weaved among the cubicles back to her own desk; her phone was ringing.

"Did he say?" asked Gilbert.

Carol glanced over her shoulder; her square-rimmed glasses magnified her milky blue eyes.

"Something about the new Jane Doe," she said.

Gilbert walked to his own desk, much larger than the one he had on Jarvis Street, and called the Office of the Chief Coroner of the Province of Ontario. Got Dr. Blackstein's voice mail. Damn. He was curious now. An identification? Maybe. One thing about the new building, it was convenient to the Coroner's Office. Blackstein was always happy to see him. He put the phone down and pulled on his coat.

He caught Lombardo standing at the security access doors next to the third-floor elevators with a couple of other young detectives; they all looked worried. And Lombardo looked more worried than the rest. His easygoing Mediterranean charm had deserted him. It wasn't the money with Joe; it was the job. He loved the work, would never want to give it up. Gilbert touched his sleeve.

"I'm going to the coroner's," he said.

Lombardo's eyes widened. "What's up?"

"Don't know," said Gilbert. "Something. You want to come?"

Lombardo shook his head. "Wish I could," he said. "I've got to see that social worker. The Wesley Rowe case?"

Gilbert's mood soured. "She's going to show you fake documentation."

"I know."

"Remember, she's not a typist, she's a social worker. You're going to see that in anything she gives you."

"I know." Lombardo glanced nervously across the atrium, where they saw Bill Marsh enter the Homicide Office. "We're going catch it, aren't we? Marsh isn't going to like this manslaughter charge, especially when the Crown is pushing for first-degree."

Gilbert frowned as he looked at Marsh. "I don't care what Marsh likes," he said. "I just care about what's fair. Get the record. I guarantee it, she's going to try something. She's fumbled, and now she's going to try to recover. Even if Wesley has to go to prison for twenty-five years."

He went the back way out, onto Grenville Street.

Out on the street the wind struck him like a fist. He pulled his collar tightly around his neck. He tried to forget about Marsh. Bay Street was clogged with the tail end of morning rush hour. The wind was so fierce he turned around, protecting his face from the sub-zero blast.

He looked at the life-size statue outside the Grenville entrance: a boy pulling a wagon; in the wagon, a large stone obelisk; on the obelisk, four words: TO SERVE, TO PROTECT. A bizarre piece. Half the detectives didn't understand it. A small boy struggling to pull a stone obelisk in his wagon. Gilbert had his own interpretation. The stone obelisk was murder; you solved murder only by the most strenuous efforts; solving murder was as hard as pulling this big stone obelisk around in a wagon.

Dr. Blackstein was in a meeting when Gilbert got to the Coroner's Building; Blackstein's assistant asked Gilbert to wait in the hall outside the morgue, told him the meeting would be over in fifteen minutes. So Gilbert went downstairs.

The hall was lit with fluorescent lights. A few snack machines stood by the fire exit.

He was just feeding some quarters into one of the machines when the elevator doors opened and out came Dr. Mervin Blackstein. He was perhaps a little older than Gilbert, but a lot shorter, with a bald pate, a black rim of hair around his head. He had a paunch and wore surgical greens and a lab-coat. Half-rim glasses sat on his prominent nose. His face was set in neither a smile nor a frown. He looked at Gilbert, his eyes even-keeled.

"Your face is red," said Dr. Blackstein.

"Have you been outside lately?" asked Gilbert.

"I don't go outside," said Blackstein. "They won't let me. I live here."

Gilbert pressed the appropriate buttons and a ham and cheese sandwich slid down the chute.

"We might as well have a look at her," said Blackstein.

The doctor took out his keys, opened the morgue door, and in they went.

Twenty-seven bodies lay on metal gurneys on either side of them, each one covered with a sheet, some with toe tags, others with scrap paper taped to gurneys: men, women, children, the latest crew of suspicious deaths.

"You've got an identification," guessed Gilbert. "Right?"

They walked to the second last gurney to the left; Blackstein pulled back the sheet.

"Do you follow politics at all?" asked Blackstein. "Did you watch any of the Provincial election on television last fall?"

Gilbert stared at the woman; she didn't look so good, now that she was starting to thaw.

"My daughters don't give me much chance at the TV," he said.

Blackstein nodded. "I think you have yourself an interesting case, Barry."

Gilbert's shoulders sank; he wished now that the woman just might remain a Jane Doe.

"Who is she?"

Blackstein gazed at the body and nodded. "Her name is Cheryl Latham. One of the attendants recognized her. She's been on TV a few times. She was a high profile campaigner for the Tories last fall. That's how the attendant recognized her." Dr. Blackstein shrugged. "Actually, she's Tom Webb's stepdaughter."

Tom Webb. Life was always full of little connections. Tom Webb, the Tory axeman, the man ultimately responsible for Homicide's eighteen-percent cut. Cheryl. She had a name now. She had an identity.

"What do you make of that gunshot wound?" asked Gilbert.

Blackstein pulled the sheet a little further down. Her flesh looked bruised down there. "I won't really know until I cut her open," said Blackstein. "But there should have been more blood. I think we have a good chance of recovering a decent slug. We'll let her thaw a bit. If I try to retrieve the slug while she's frozen like this, I might damage it." He pulled the sheet over Cheryl Latham's face and looked up at Gilbert. "I guess you better make an appointment to see Tom Webb."

The Ontario Legislative Building—the province's seat of power—stood at the top of University Avenue in Queen's

Park. The nineteenth-century building with its multitude of wings was of some architectural interest, especially to Gilbert, who had taken two years of architectural school before going into police work.

After leaving the Coroner's Building, he walked west along Grenville Street. This took him directly to the east side of the Parliament Buildings. As he waited for the cars to pass, he looked up at the impressive landmark. As an architectural buff, he knew a thing or two about the building. Built in the 1890s, it was a Romanesque revival extravaganza made from ruddy red stone cut from quarries in and around the Credit Valley. Arches, buttresses, and turrets proliferated. The Canadian and Ontario flags snapped briskly in the cold north wind out front.

The traffic cleared and Gilbert walked across the street into the grounds. Some health-care workers were gathered with pickets by the main portico to protest the latest round of cuts. He couldn't help noticing the words on one of the pickets: STOP THE WEBB OF DECEIT. He shook his head. Webb might have been the Premier's axeman, but he was also Willis' lightning rod. He passed the statue of Queen Victoria, hurried up the steps, and entered the spacious main hall.

He checked his watch. Nearly one. The Legislative Assembly would be breaking for lunch soon; his appointment with Webb was at one-fifteen. He showed a uniformed legislative security officer his shield and asked where he might find Webb's office.

"Second floor, west wing, near the end," said the officer.

Gilbert climbed the stairs, his footsteps muffled on the thick red carpet. Paintings hung everywhere, old ones, portraits of politicians and generals from Ontario's colonial past, and a particularly large one of Canada's Fathers of Confederation above the large entrance to the Legislative Library. He glanced up at the panoply of foliage carved into the sycamore and mahogany trim. He hairpinned around the banister and climbed the next set of stairs. As he passed the doors of the Legislative Chamber, he heard the province's parliamentarians pontificating within; a tattoo of bench slapping erupted; an honorable member was trying to shout over this bench slapping, pleading with the Speaker to bring the House to order. Gilbert shook his head and continued on.

He ventured into the west wing, past the white marbled colonnades, and soon came to the office of the chairman of the management board, the cabinet position Webb occupied, his name in gold lettering on frosted glass. He pushed the heavy mahogany door open and was greeted by a receptionist, a young woman with dark shoulder-length hair, pale green eyes, a complexion as fair as porcelain. Gilbert showed her his shield.

"I'm here to see Mr. Webb," he said. "I have an appointment at one-fifteen."

The woman glanced at his badge, lifted the phone, dialed an in-house extension, and paused.

"Jane?" said the woman. "Detective Gilbert is here. Should I send him in?"

Another pause. Gilbert looked around the office. Six or seven cubicles made up the central area; several doorways led to numerous separate offices, and through an open door in the corner he saw an empty meeting room, appointed in dark mahogany, with red carpeting, a large meeting table, and several chairs hobnailed with red leather. Various assistants and secretaries busied themselves at computer terminals.

"Thanks, Jane." The woman put the phone down. "Jane will be out in a minute," she said. "If you just want to take a seat."

"Thanks."

He took off his coat and scarf, hung them on an antique coat-tree, and sat down.

A minute later, a woman in her mid-forties emerged from one of the offices, a bright public-relations smile on her face.

"Detective Gilbert?" she said. "I'm Jane Ireland, Mr. Webb's personal secretary. If you'd like to wait in his office."

She was attractive, slim, wore a deep blue outfit with imposing shoulders and rigorous business-like lines, a suit that spoke of power and influence. Though her lips were rather small, and her chin and brow somewhat pronounced, she nonetheless had pleasing blue eyes. Her hair was a deep chestnut brown. He was surprised by how thick her wrists were, strong wrists, mannish wrists, as if she did a lot of heavy lifting.

"I'm a little early," said Gilbert.

"That's all right," said Ms. Ireland, as if nothing could make her happier. "Just follow me."

She turned and walked with prim steps, leading him to the office.

The Minister's office consisted of two rooms; the outer reception room, where Jane Ireland had her desk and computer, and the inner office, Tom Webb's office. As she closed the door, the smile slipped from Ms. Ireland's face like leaves from a maple in fall.

"What's happened?" she asked.

Gilbert's face settled. He could appreciate Jane Ireland's concern, how she wanted to protect her boss.

"I'm afraid I better talk to Mr. Webb," he said.

She stared at him, her bright blue eyes unwavering. Gilbert was perplexed. Her eyes glistened; she lifted her chin, gave it a small involuntary shake, then took a deep breath. Did she know something?

"I've sent a page to the Chamber," she said. "He knows you're here." Her voice was no longer bright. She opened the door to the inner office. "You might as well wait in there."

Now she wouldn't look at him. He couldn't decide. Did she look guilty? Or was she just anxious?

"Thanks," he said.

He entered the office and she closed the door partway behind him.

The office was large, as befitted a preeminent member of the Conservative Cabinet, with sixteen-foot ceilings, a desk as big as a king-size bed, sofas, chairs, a table, a private bar, a private washroom, and a stunning view of University Avenue, where the financial spires rose into the brittle February sunshine. A fireplace stood against the north wall, intricately carved with Victorian scrollwork. Several paintings hung on the wall, all of them landscapes—silver birch, pine, rock, and lake—pictures of northern Ontario. Five photographs stood on the mantelpiece. One showed Tom Webb, a silver-haired man, six-feet-five, in a blue pin-striped business suit, wearing a Remembrance Day poppy, taking the oath of office last November. The others were just portraits. Three he didn't recognize, probably family members, but the fourth was none other than Cheryl Latham. He took a closer look.

She was younger in this photograph, maybe by a year or two. She wore a wedding gown and her hair was fixed in an arrangement of lace and lilies-of-the-valley. A wedding photograph. But where was the husband? Certainly not on this mantelpiece. He was again struck by the innocence of her face, her delicate pixie-like features, the earnestness of her blue eyes, the genuine honesty of her smile, the golden lustre of her hair. Her freckles gave her a girlish look. Yet now that he looked closer, he sensed a darker quality to those eyes, as if beneath her honesty she was trying to hide something. Who was her husband? Who was Mr. Latham? And if Tom Webb was Cheryl Latham's stepfather, where and who was her real father?

"Detective Gilbert?"

He turned around. Tom Webb stood in the doorway. Here was the man responsible for Homicide's eighteen-percent cut. Yet Gilbert felt no antipathy toward the man. Webb looked older than he did in the newspapers and on television. His presence was imposing. His silver hair was thick, his face narrow, handsome, and after a week of sailing his catamaran in the Caribbean, deeply tanned. Gilbert showed him his shield. Webb didn't look at it.

"Sit down, detective." An order, not an invitation.

"Mr. Webb, I'm afraid I have some bad news." The expression on Webb's face did not change; he looked mystified; his eyes seemed both dull and unaware. "Maybe you should be the one to sit down."

But Webb remained standing. Was the man on drugs? Why such an oblivious look in his eyes? Webb shoved the door closed.

"Detective, I'm a busy man."

Gilbert shrugged. If that's the way he wanted it.

"We found your stepdaughter murdered this morning down at Dominion Malting," he said.

Webb's eyes shifted, glanced downward at the Persian carpet, a gift from the emir of Kuwait, and his shoulders sagged; his lips parted, exposing long upper teeth, and he nodded a few times, an infinitesimally small jerking of his head as he absently slid his hands into pockets. He turned his head suddenly to one side and took a sharp breath, as if he had just been punched in the solar plexus. He stepped toward his desk, two steps in all, stopped, stared at the green blotter, then slowly turned back to Gilbert, peering at Gilbert from under his sleek silver brow.

"We got the call at seven o'clock this morning," said Gilbert, feeling he had to add something. "The security guard down there found her."

"Are you sure it's her?"

The obliviousness left Webb's eyes and he no longer looked like a politician; he looked nearly human. This was what they all asked. Gilbert nodded.

"It's her," he said. "We'll need you to come to the Coroner's Office to make an official identification."

He looked momentarily annoyed. "I'm in committee all afternoon."

Maybe not so human after all.

"Perhaps your wife can—"

"My wife's been dead for three years."

"What about Cheryl's husband?"

"Charles and Cheryl have been separated for over a year."

"Are there any siblings?"

"No. Cheryl's the only . . ." Webb looked at his watch. "I can come at three. Can we do it at three?"

"I'll make sure somebody's there," said Gilbert.

They stood there in silence. Webb no longer looked annoyed. Outside, Gilbert heard the health-care workers chanting: "Hey-hey, ho-ho, Thomas Webb has got to go." Webb looked at the large arched windows and a faint grin came to his face.

"Listen to them," he said.

Gilbert thought Webb might elaborate; but he continued to stare at the cold February sunshine streaming through the windows, finally took a few steps, sat on the edge of his desk, clasped his hand together, and glanced at Gilbert.

"Look, I think I better be alone for a minute or . . . Cheryl and I weren't exactly close but I . . ."

"I understand," said Gilbert. But he made no move toward the door. "We might need your help with this, Mr. Webb."

"Let's not make a media circus of it, okay?"

"If the media get wind of it, it won't be from our side."

"What do you need to know?"

"Where she lives, for one thing. Where she works. Where her ex-husband lives."

"I have no idea where Charles lives."

"Okay. But anything else you think might be of use to us."

He shrugged, and now a distant look came to his eyes, as if he were running old memories through his head. "You can leave your card with Jane," said Webb. He looked at Gilbert. "Would that be all right? I'll have her phone over the information once we dig it up."

"That would be fine," said Gilbert. He took out his wallet and extracted his card. Then he peered at Webb; he nearly got the sense that Webb was relieved in some way. "Do you have any idea who might have wanted to kill Cheryl?" he asked.

Webb again stared out the window; the decibel level of the protesters outside was rising. No one, it seemed, in the whole Province of Ontario, wanted to take an eighteen-percent cut.

"None," said Webb. "None whatsoever."

"Do you have time for a few questions?"

Webb's eyes settled on Gilbert like two balls of ice. "I'm afraid we're right in the middle of session back in the Chamber," he said. "I don't think there's anything further I can add right now." He stood up and gestured toward the door. "Jane will phone when she gets a moment."

Chapter Three

Gilbert picked up Lombardo at the Murray Street entrance of the Mount Joseph General Hospital an hour later. Lombardo carried a large manila envelope. As he slid into the passenger seat, Lombardo held up the envelope in a gesture of triumph.

"You should see them," he said. "Typos all over the place."

"I told you so." Gilbert swung out onto Murray Street and made a quick left on Orde. "What about format?"

"All social work reports are run through a Lasotec laser printer up in Medical Records." Lombardo tapped the envelope. "These were done on a typewriter."

Gilbert grinned. "I told you," he said. "And I bet her story's different now. I bet it says she now requested home care. I bet she deemed Wesley unfit to look after his mother. Did you get the Medical Records transcription logs?"

"They're in the envelope," said Lombardo. "There's no record that these new notes were ever dictated. We've got her, Barry. We've got her."

*   *   *

They pulled in front of Cheryl Latham's apartment building a short while later; though it was just past four, the sky was already dark, and a blurry swath of snow-bearing clouds spilled from the northwest like a can of grey paint. The temperature remained cold, but at least the wind had died down. They found a parking space a few doors away, got out, and walked the remaining distance.

Gilbert glanced around.

Her building was nestled among older four-bedroom two-storey homes, an anomaly in this neighborhood of single-family dwellings. They climbed the steps and entered the foyer. He looked up, saw a security monitor, its red light flashing.

"Look at that," he said.

Lombardo nodded. "I'll get the tapes," he said.

They rang Percy Waxman's buzzer.

A minute later they watched the superintendent walk down the hall, a short man with long arms, stooped shoulders, and a shuffling but nonetheless long stride; the effect was ape-like. He gave them a wave through the netted glass door. Three paint scrapers poked from his shirt pocket, there was a pencil stuck behind his ear, and he was dressed in grey—grey workman's trousers and a grey shirt with his name embroidered in gold on a small cloth badge above the right breast.

He opened the door and let them in. "You're late," he said. He spoke with a faint Polish accent. "I was just about to leave." They stepped inside; the hall looked freshly painted, was brightly lit with small chandeliers. The air smelled of lemon household cleanser. Waxman turned abruptly, as if he had wasted too much time already, and led them down the hall, not once looking back.

Gilbert and Lombardo glanced at each other.

"Mr. Waxman," said Gilbert, "we have a consent-to-search

form we'd like you to sign." Gilbert snapped open his accordion-style briefcase, an heirloom from his father, and pulled out the form. "Just put your signature here, and we'll go up."

Lombardo pulled a pen from his pocket and offered it to Waxman.

Waxman stopped, turned around, and looked at them with irritable eyes.

"Sign where?" he said, feverish with impatience.

Gilbert showed him the spot.

He scribbled his signature quickly, as if he just wanted to get the whole thing over with, gave the form back, then continued down the hall.

He led them through a set of double glass doors to a stairwell.

"Can we ask a few questions?" said Gilbert, as they began to climb the stairs.

"Ask away," said Waxman. He wouldn't look back at them; it was as if he believed both detectives carried the plague.

"Did she have many visitors?" asked Lombardo.

"I don't know," he said. "How would I know? She's on the fourth floor. I'm on the first. You think I have X-ray vision?"

They hairpinned around the first landing and proceeded up the next flight.

"How long has she been living here?" asked Gilbert.

"A year."

"Can you check that?" suggested Lombardo.

"I don't need to," said Waxman. "I know it's a year."

"Does she have any friends in the building?" asked Gilbert.

Waxman pulled a paint scraper from his pocket, scraped a suspicious piece of dirt from the tile steps, and put it into his pocket.

"She sometimes talked to Sonia," he said. "They did their laundry together."

"Who's Sonia?" asked Lombardo.

"In 4F," said Waxman. He stopped, listened: the pipes behind the walls clanked as the boiler surged. "I wish I could fix that," he said. He shrugged and continued up the stairs.

They reached the fourth floor a moment later. At the end of the corridor, Gilbert saw a fire door.

"Is that fire door rigged to an alarm?" he asked.

"Yes," said Waxman.

"Is it regularly inspected?" asked Lombardo.

"Just last month," said Waxman.

"So if I open it, the bell starts ringing," said Lombardo.

"What did I just say?" said Waxman.

"Are the fire escape and the front door the only way in and out?" asked Lombardo, unfazed by Waxman.

"You could jump." Waxman looked back at Joe, as if he hoped Joe might take his suggestion literally.

Gilbert and Lombardo again looked at each other. Waxman was one of those guys.

At the end of the hall, Waxman unhooked his keys from his belt and opened the door. He took a brief glance in, didn't seem too interested, then looked back at the detectives. "Get me when you're finished," he said. "I'll be in the office. You're not going to tape it or anything, are you? I just put fresh paint on last month."

Gilbert sighed. "It depends, Mr. Waxman."

"On what?"

"On whether it's a crime scene or not. We won't know that until we take a look."

Waxman gave them a sullen nod, not at all pleased. "Try to be careful," he said. "I try to keep things nice around here."

Waxman turned and padded away. Gilbert and Lombardo

stared at him. Gilbert finally shrugged. "I think we just about ruined his day," he said.

They pulled on cloth gardening gloves, opened the door, checked the entranceway first, no sign of forced entry, then went inside.

Kitchen to the right, living room to the left, a dining nook at right angles to the living room just beyond the kitchen.

What Gilbert noticed first and foremost was the dead parrot lying on the living room floor. Who wouldn't? A lot of books had been pulled from bookshelves, many lying open face down in haphazard piles. He took a few steps into the room and crouched beside the dead parrot. Lombardo came up behind. Gilbert stared at the parrot. Bright French green. A South American parrot. With some red and yellow head feathers, and white skin around the eyes. A black beak. Some matted blood in the wing feathers. A tropical apparition on this cold February afternoon.

"Did you see the sign out front?" said Gilbert.

"What sign?" asked Lombardo.

Gilbert stood up. "No pets," he said.

They split up: Lombardo went to the kitchen while Gilbert stayed in the living room.

Books on the floor, but also old LPs taken from the shelf under the Technics turntable, each vinyl disk pulled from its sleeve and left in a rough pile on the floor. Mostly classical music. Bach, Telemann, Handel. Somebody had tossed the place. The slipcovers on the couch pillows had been unzipped and the foam rubber partially pulled out. He turned on the brass floor lamp. The parrot's bamboo cage stood in the corner, its door open, bird seed scattered on the floor below. Who would kill a parrot? Why kill a parrot? And having a parrot for a pet, what did that say about Cheryl Latham? Some of the desk drawers were open, and the contents looked gone through. Whoever searched this apartment took care not to disturb it more than necessary. Could he reasonably conclude that whoever had searched this apartment had also killed Cheryl Latham? He shook his head. He couldn't conclude anything yet. Maybe Cheryl herself had been searching for something.

Prints and paintings had been pulled from the wall, the paper backings cut off the frame with a sharp implement, the paintings then neatly stacked against the balcony door. Outside, fresh snowflakes batted at the window. Books opened, LPs removed from jacket sleeves, the paper backing removed from prints and paintings, the slipcovers unzipped. Searching for something flat, something that could be hid in those places. Cash? Was this just a straight-ahead murder-robbery? No. He looked at the dead parrot again. Not a robbery. Not with her body down at Dominion Malting. But if not cash, then what?

"Anything in the kitchen?" he called.

"You should see how well she's got this organized," called Lombardo.

Gilbert walked to the kitchen. In the glass cupboard the glasses were lined up in even rows, like a battalion of soldiers, each one exactly the same distance from the next, each one identical so that the impression of uniformity was overwhelming. Copper-bottomed pots, seven in all, hung on hooks next to the refrigerator, each one dazzlingly clean, the largest on the far left, the smallest on the far right, the middle ones arranged in a diminishing sequence of size.

"And look at this," said Lombardo, opening one of the cupboards under the counter.

Canned goods. Arranged in a series of diminishing concentric circles on a lazy Susan, the small cans on the outside, the large ones in the middle. On the shelf below, bottles of wine in a small wine rack. Small handwritten labels had been affixed to the corked spout of each bottle, telling what each one was.

"That's excessive," said Lombardo.

"Just because you drink your father's rotgut all the time doesn't mean you have to criticize," said Gilbert.

"My father doesn't make rotgut."

"I know. He makes vinegar."

"I thought you said you liked his last batch," said Lombardo.

"I did," said Gilbert. "I had a clogged drain and it worked beautifully."

Gilbert opened the cupboard under the sink, where a wire frame with a flip-top lid held a small garbage bag in place. He looked under the sink; various cleaning products stood in a neat row. From the corner of his eye he noticed a single reddish-brown drip mark on the rubber-coated wire frame of the garbage bag holder, hidden behind the garbage bag. Except for this single drip mark, which anybody, even Cheryl could have missed, the cupboard gleamed. Gilbert pointed.

"Look at this," he said.

"That's blood," said Lombardo.

They both stared at the small saber-shaped drip. Then Gilbert stood up, put his hands on his hips, and took a deep breath. Outside, the wind was building, whistling through the blue spruces in the next yard.

"We'll call Forensic," said Gilbert. "We'll have them scrape it off. It looks like a good sample. Go have a look at the living room, tell me what you think. I'll check the bedroom and bathroom."

"What do you think they were looking for?" asked Lombardo.

"I don't know," said Gilbert. "Something flat. Paper? Cash? Something that would fit in a book or a cushion."

"Do you think they found it?"

"We'll have to see if the bedroom's been searched."

Gilbert left the kitchen.

He entered the bedroom. The bed had been pushed to one side, the blankets disturbed, as if they'd been pulled away, then put roughly back into place. The mattress rested askew on the box spring; somebody must have looked under it. The rug had been rolled up. He opened the dresser drawers; the women's underthings, the sweaters, the sweatpants, the socks—all looked gone through. Cheryl's wallet sat on top of the dresser along with two framed photographs. He opened the wallet. Two-hundred-and-sixty dollars, a driver's license, two major credit cards. Not a robbery. A thief would have gone for the easy cash and credit cards. He looked at the photographs. One was a graduation photograph of Cheryl, she must have been twenty-one, a fleshier rounder face, wearing a mortar board and graduation gown, her blonde hair longer, straighter, brighter. The other showed a younger Cheryl, fifteen years old, standing beside an old woman—was it her mother?—and a girl of maybe twelve. They posed in front of a wood shack in the middle of winter. The young girl held up a two-foot pickerel. Ice fishing? Who was this girl? A sister? She bore no resemblance to Cheryl. Cheryl had a certain snap; this girl was dull, had a small ferret-like face and bad teeth.

He lifted the telephone on the bedside table, pulled out his notebook, and dialed Bell Canada's last-number service, *69. The computerized voice gave Gilbert the last number Cheryl had called; he scribbled it in his notebook. Then he dialed the operator and had her connect him to the name-that-number service. He quoted the number. He didn't have to write down the name when the service operator gave him the answer; it was already there under his potential suspects list: Charles Latham, Cheryl's ex-husband.

He put the receiver down and went into the bathroom. The door was cracked, the wood trim around the jamb broken, the tile floor powdered with plaster dust. The medicine cabinet mirror was broken, with several of the lower shards leaning out from the frame. A struggle? The door forced, the mirror broken. He tried to discern footprints in the plaster dust, but the dust was much too disturbed. He looked at the hall floor. By rights, there should have been plaster dust tracked out there. But the hardwood floor was spotless. Someone had cleaned up afterward. The wastepaper basket lay on its side. It was full of unused toilet paper. Taken from the roll and simply dumped in the basket in a long curving ribbon. He lifted the wastepaper basket. Something heavy shifted within the folds of toilet paper. Moving the tissue carefully aside, he saw the handset from a General Electric cordless phone. The handset didn't look damaged in any way. So why would it be in the wastepaper basket underneath all that toilet paper? He pressed the engage button; he got a dial tone. It was working. He put the phone back in the basket, lowered the basket to the floor, and made a note.

And he noticed more blood. Two drops, about an inch apart, in an oblong pattern that suggested the splatters came from the direction of the sink. He knelt and closed the shut-off valves; Forensic would have to check the catch-pipe. He stood up and tapped the end of his pen against his notebook. Was Cheryl Latham murdered here, in this apartment? He didn't think so. In such a quiet building, in such a quiet neighborhood, the shot would have been heard.

He reviewed the security tape from the Glenarden down at College Street with Percy Waxman just after seven that night.

Because it had been such a cold night, people entering the Glenarden on the night of the murder had been thoroughly bundled. Four wore parkas with deep hoods; Waxman was unable to identify them. Three others, all men, wore balaclavas. Waxman couldn't identify these either.

"Can I go now?" asked Waxman.

Gilbert looked at the man.

"I don't want anyone going into her apartment under any circumstances," said Gilbert.

"Do we have to have the crime-scene tape across the door?"

"Yes, we do."

"How long will it be there. It looks like hell."

"As long as it takes," said Gilbert.

He let Waxman go. As long as it takes. But this wasn't a dunker. This wasn't a grounder, something he could easily throw to home plate. This was a pop fly. This was out of the ballpark. This was a whodunit and a mystery. Even worse, this was a heavy, a powder keg, and, under the circumstances of the flagging clearance rates, with budget cuts on the way, couldn't have come at a worse time. His stomach growled. He should really go home to Regina. These sixteen-hour days were starting to get to him. But he had to make Joe Lombardo look good on this one. Because he had a feeling Marsh had zeroed in on Joe. He had to show Marsh just what a good detective Joe could be. He wanted to save Joe's job on this one. Because he really suspected Joe's job was in danger. And that was too bad because if anyone was meant to be a homicide detective, Joe Lombardo was; the facts he unearthed behind the scenes were often stupendous.

Gilbert rolled back the tape to some marked off counter numbers, then pressed play.

There she was, Cheryl Latham, coming home from work at 6:15 last night. Fast-forward. There she was leaving, at 7:02, wearing running shoes, exercise tights, and a green parka. Fast-forward. Here she was, coming back again at 9:16. And that was it. According to the security tape, she didn't leave the building after 9:16. Yet she was found this morning at Dominion Malting, frozen solid, like one of those ancient victims at Pompeii so many centuries ago. With the front stairs and fire escape the only way in or out, just how the hell did she wind up down at the pier?

Chapter Four

At the morgue the next morning, an hour after Cheryl Latham's autopsy, Gilbert entered Dr. Blackstein's office with two coffees to talk things over. He sat in one of two chairs in front of Blackstein's desk. Blackstein sat behind his desk glancing over the business-size sheets of the preliminary report. Outside his window a few pigeons huddled on his sill, trying to keep warm. Today was just as cold as yesterday, and the weatherman wasn't predicting milder temperatures until the weekend.

Dr. Blackstein lifted a small zip-lock glassine bag. "Here's your slug," he said. "I've made a notation in the evidence log. It's yours now. It looks like a .45 to me, but you can have your ballistics check it out."

Gilbert took the bag and had a close look at the bullet. "That's not so good, is it?" he said. "A soft-nose. It mushroomed more than usual. Ballistics aren't going to have much to work with."

Dr. Blackstein shook his head. "Not so soft. You saw the

area of cavitation around the wound downstairs?" Gilbert nodded. "I've thought about it now. It was much shallower than usual. And the hydrostatic shock was much smaller as well." Dr. Blackstein shrugged. "And that can mean only one thing. She was already frozen when your perp shot her. She was already dead. You've got a screwball, Barry," he said.

Gilbert stared at the bullet. "Overkill?" he suggested.

"I don't know," said Blackstein. "It's not like the usual overkill we see. With real overkill, your perp would have emptied his clip. You saw how we dug around. We found only the one slug."

Why would anyone shoot a person who was already dead?

"So she froze to death," he said.

"The change in blood gases confirms it."

"So maybe she wasn't murdered. Maybe she just froze to death."

"You've still got manslaughter," said Dr. Blackstein.

"If not second-degree."

Dr. Blackstein rested his hands on top of the preliminary report. "Like I said, I think we have a screwball. Your perp didn't actively kill her. He let the elements do it for him."

Gilbert nodded. "That's murder," he said. "Whether we can prove it . . ." He took a sip of his coffee and nodded at the preliminary report. "What else did you put down?"

"Pretty well everything I said downstairs while you were watching us," said Blackstein. He glanced at the report, summarizing. "A single contusion to the right side of the head. Glass slivers recovered from her hair. She was wearing contact lenses. She wears a bridge; her front teeth are false. There's an old scar on her lower lip. It looks like she had her teeth bashed out at some time in her life. Lungs and heart were fine. Her stomach contents consisted of coffee and half digested jelly donut. Also some salad. The bullet penetrated the upper intestine." Blackstein flipped to the last page of the provisional autopsy report, where there was a crude drawing of a woman's body. "Right here," said Blackstein, tapping an X in the drawing's abdomen. "There's an upward trajectory of maybe thirty degrees."

Gilbert inspected the drawing.

"What are these little stroke marks all over the arms, the ribs, and the head."

Blackstein peered over his glasses. His phone rang but he let his voice mail get it.

"The X-ray came back," he said. "These are multiple distant fractures. She had a lot of accidents as a kid. If you can find some relatives, maybe you should check these out. Three times she broke her right arm. Twice her left. Seven broken ribs at various times in life. A fractured skull. And there's scar tissue all over her spleen. Accidents like that . . . well, statistically, it's way out of line. A kid shouldn't have that many accidents." The doctor squinted and shook his head. "What can I tell you, Barry? I think she was beaten as a child. We have the missing teeth, and all this other stuff." Blackstein took a sip of coffee and looked out the window. The pigeons on the sill jumped into the air and took off in the direction of Yonge Street. He shook his head again. "Someone beat the crap out of that woman when she was a kid."

Gilbert met Sonia Bailey, Cheryl Latham's Glenarden neighbor, on her lunch hour at Cultures, a buffet-style restaurant downtown. She was a tall, exceedingly attractive mulatto from Antigua who worked as an executive secretary at Canada Life in the historic old building south of the Royal Canadian Military Institute. She ordered vegetarian chili with tofu. Gilbert had the meat lasagna. The place was full of office and hospital workers grabbing a quick lunch. Because it was so cold outside, the large windows had steamed over; someone had drawn a face in the misty coating.

Sonia Bailey was subdued; she'd learned of the murder just this morning. She had an open and honest nut-brown face with dark searching eyes. She leaned forward, wanting only to help.

"How long did you know Cheryl?" asked Gilbert.

She glanced up at the low-slung halogen lamps. "A year," she said. "Maybe a bit more." She spoke with a musical West Indian accent.

"Did you know her well?" asked Gilbert.

She considered this. "I knew her better than I know any of the other tenants. She was my neighbor. We talked when we met in the hall. We did our laundry together. We had dinner together twice, and coffee down at Starbucks a few times. I'm not sure I got to know her that well. She seemed a private person."

Out on University Avenue two pumper trucks from the local firehouse roared by; in this cold weather, the buildup of static electricity in Mount Sinai Hospital was constantly setting the alarms off.

"Did she ever talk about Charles?" asked Gilbert.

"Her husband?" she said, arching her delicate brows. "Once."

"And what did she say?"

"That she was separated, that she was filing for divorce."

"That's it?"

She nodded. "That's it."

"Did you ever meet Charles?"

"No."

A man sat down at the next table with a bowl of vegetable chowder and two slices of sourdough bread; he opened a small laptop computer and called up some graphs to the screen.

"Did you ever see her with anyone else? Did you ever hear anyone else in her apartment with her?"

"No. She never had visitors. At least not when I was there." Sonia twisted her lips to one side, as if she were recalling something. "Wait a minute," she said. "I saw her once with a Chinese woman. I guess she must have been a friend. She was helping Cheryl up the stairs with a new armchair."

"And how long ago was this?"

Sonia shrugged. "Six months. Maybe seven."

"Do you know the woman's name?"

"No. I passed them in the stairwell. I was in a hurry. We just said hello."

"What did this Chinese woman look like?"

"She was pretty. Slim. About five-seven. She had her bangs trimmed straight above her eyebrows."

"How old?"

"Early thirties."

Gilbert glanced at the man's laptop screen; the man was moving things around with the trackball and drag key. Laptop for lunch. Gilbert knew the feeling. He sawed into his meat lasagna and chewed. A Chinese woman. A thin lead, but it would have to be checked out.

"Did she ever talk about her family?" he asked. "Did she ever mention her stepfather?"

"Tom Webb?" Sonia took a sip of her carrot juice and glanced at her watch. "No, never."

"Did she ever mention her real father? Her biological father?"

"No."

"Or any siblings?"

"I think she has a sister. But she lives up north. Somewhere around Sudbury."

"Is that where Cheryl's from?" Gilbert thought of the photograph on Cheryl's dresser; the woman and the girl and the ice-fishing shack.

"I don't know. She never said where she came from."

Easy enough getting answers from Sonia Bailey. But the answers seemed to have little value.

"Have you noticed anything odd about Cheryl's behavior in the last little while?" he asked.

Sonia lifted her hand and waved to somebody she knew, a balding man with a beard wearing a Hudson Bay tricolor parka, just coming in from the cold.

"Not really," she said. But then her brow furrowed. "Unless . . ."

Gilbert waited. "Unless what?"

Sonia's eyes seemed to focus on some undefinable point. But then she looked at Gilbert full in the face. "I found her crying in the laundry room once. In fact, not too long ago. Maybe about two weeks ago. She wouldn't tell me what it was about, only that she was remembering something sad. That's out of character for Cheryl. She's always so happy. She's always humming. She never gets down about anything. I thought she must have been sick. I told her she should see a doctor but she said no, she would be all right, she just needed a little time to sort things out." Sonia Bailey dipped her spoon into her chili. "She never told me what she meant by that. I just left her alone. I thought that was best."

Back at headquarters, Joe Lombardo had the ballistics results from the recovered slug.

"The lands and grooves were in good shape, despite the slug's condition," he said. Lombardo pointed to the flowering cactus on Gilbert's window ledge. "Is that new?" he asked.

Gilbert gazed at the bright vermilion bloom on top of the prickly tuber.

"Valerie gave me that."

Lombardo nodded, but it was a cagey nod, a nod that jock-eyed for position. "Valerie," he said. "The girl from Denmark. The exchange student."

"She's from Germany."

"How can I find out about that? I've got the extra room at my place. I'd love to have an exchange student stay with me for a while."

Gilbert stared at Lombardo skeptically. "I bet you would."

"No, I'm serious."

"The only reason she's here is because Jennifer spent six weeks in Germany last summer."

"So I have to have my own daughter first?"

"You'd have to talk to Regina. She arranged it all."

Lombardo grinned. "But I don't think Regina wants any more children. And isn't she already married?"

Gilbert made a face. "Some day I'm going to have to reform you."

"I thought you already had."

"You won't recognize yourself once I get through with you."

"If I end up anything like you, I won't want to recognize myself."

Gilbert now grinned back. "You'd like being me," he said. "You'd be able to have exchange students stay with you."

Lombardo laughed.

"Now what do you got on this bullet?" asked Gilbert.

Lombardo looked down at the ballistics report. "A Heckler and Koch .45 semiautomatic with a copper sheath."

"That narrows it."

"And I've got Laird's list. He's got thirteen cars. He also cautions that the Michelin XGT is a popular replacement tire."

"Shit."

"I know."

Gilbert tapped his desk a few times. "Did you dig around in marriage records at all?" he asked.

Lombardo nodded. "Cheryl's been married only the once. To Charles Latham."

"No, I'm talking about her mother. Doris."

"It's actually Dorothy," said Lombardo. "I had to make a few calls." Lombardo slid his hands into the pockets of his stylish pleated pants. "She died three years ago from breast cancer. Tom Webb was actually her third husband, Cheryl's second stepdad. Before Tom Webb, she was married to a man named Paul Varley, no details, only that he died some time in the early 1970s. Before that, Dorothy was married to a mid-level mining executive, Craig Shaw, who worked for Lac Minerals in Sudbury. He was killed while on a tour of one of their newly sunk shafts in Povungnituk, Quebec. Cheryl must have been seven at the time."

"So Cheryl's from Sudbury?"

"They actually lived in Laurentian Hills. That's a well-to-do suburb just outside Sudbury. Tom Webb's riding is up there, Sudbury West. I guess Dorothy met Webb up there."

Gilbert stared at the paperweight of bullet slugs McEndoo had fashioned for him down in the machine shop.

"Any siblings?"

"Not from that first marriage," said Lombardo. "Cheryl was an only child. But Paul Varley had three kids, two boys and a girl. Nothing much on her step siblings yet, just their birth records. Larry and Dean are the boys. Donna's the girl."

"Webb should have told me this."

"Maybe he doesn't know. Maybe Dorothy never told him."

Gilbert raised his eyebrows. That might be a possibility.

"I guess we'll have to get in touch with them," Gilbert said. He lifted the bullet paperweight and turned it on its side. "Does the name sound familiar to you?"

"What name?"

"Varley."

Lombardo cocked his head. "No," he said. "Should it?"

Gilbert shook his head to himself. "I don't know." He put the paperweight down. "Maybe . . . no, I guess not. But I can't help . . ."

Lombardo shrugged. "Do you want me to get some sandwiches or something?"

But Gilbert hardly listened. Varley. He filed it away, then looked up at Lombardo.

"Any make on the blood yet?"

Lombardo nodded. "The stuff we found on the bathroom floor was Cheryl's. The stuff under the kitchen sink . . ." Lombardo took his hands out of his pockets and put them on his hips. "Well . . . it's somebody else's."

"Mystery blood."

"You guessed it."

"What about the hair?"

"It's not Cheryl's. That's about as far as we've got."

"Anything new from Dominion Malting?"

A sudden wind blew a snow squall against the pane.

"Fifty-two Division's gone over and over it. Either the ejected cartridge has been lost, or the perp took it with him when he left."

Chapter Five

Early the next day, with the shift barely an hour old, and the sky still dark on yet another frigidly cold February morning, Staff Inspector Bill Marsh called Detective-Sergeant Barry Gilbert into his office. The Staff Inspector's office overlooked the police courtyard, with a view of the old YMCA below. A large man to begin with, Marsh looked even larger in this small office. The desktop computer had been relegated to a shelf. A Smith-Corona electric typewriter, veteran of a thousand murder cases, as battered and war-scarred as Marsh, sat front and center.

"Two things, Barry," said Marsh.

A stack of case file folders sat at Marsh's elbow; Gilbert recognized most of the numbers as his own, open homicides from the last three months. Gilbert waited.

"I got a call last night as I was going home," said Marsh. "From Deputy Chief Ling. He was asking about the Cheryl Latham case. He wants to know if you've developed a suspect yet."

Gilbert glanced at Marsh's shelf full of bowling trophies. "Bill, it's been two days."

"That's our usual envelope."

"We have some ideas. Whether they'll pan out remains to be seen."

"Isn't that kind of vague?"

"We're still gathering evidence."

Through the open door of Marsh's office Gilbert saw Carol Reid; she glanced their way, smelling blood.

"Not good enough, Barry. I want a name."

"I'm not prepared to give you a name. If I give you a name, you're going to run with it. And I don't think we're at the running stage yet."

Marsh leaned forward, putting his beefy forearms on the table; his chrome accordion-style watchband glittered in the overhead fluorescent light.

"This is high profile, Barry. You know it is."

"No one's told the press."

"Don't be so sure. Ling's pushing me. He's looking at the statistics."

"Let him look all he likes. Those statistics mean nothing."

"But this is Tom Webb's stepdaughter."

"I know that."

"And Webb was seen at the Coroner's Building yesterday."

"That's procedure."

"No. I mean he was *seen*."

Gilbert's eyes narrowed; Marsh's anxiety was always contagious. "Seen by whom?" asked Gilbert.

"By Ronald Roffey."

"Does he follow me wherever I go?" asked Gilbert.

"The idiot's going to print something," said Marsh. "He wants to know why Tom Webb was at the Coroner's Building yesterday."

Gilbert took a deep breath. He shrugged. "It was just a

matter of time, Bill. I think we better start working on a statement."

"Okay, okay." Marsh's face reddened. "That's my first point. Now for my second point."

"Which is?"

Gilbert contemplated Marsh. As usual, Marsh seemed annoyed by the whole world; he believed he was surrounded by invisible enemies. And whenever Marsh felt surrounded by invisible enemies, he picked on people. It was Gilbert's turn today.

Marsh took a sip of his coffee. "Don't get me wrong, Barry, I like you, I think your work is stellar, but sometimes I think you get a little too creative. You got to take a simpler approach. Second point, Wesley Rowe. Here you got enough evidence to nail the guy for first-degree murder, and he's still out walking the streets."

"He's in a co-op, Bill." Gilbert began to get a sour feeling inside. "He's not going to run. He's mentally incompetent. He wouldn't know how to run even if you showed him the road."

"You got blood all over the place, you got an axe in his mother's head, and you got the guy sitting on the front steps waiting for the police to come. He actually takes them upstairs to the crime scene."

"Yeah, but consider the extenuating circumstances, Bill. He's forty years old and he's never done more than rake leaves or mow lawns for pocket change. He can't even spell his own name. He's lived with his mother all his life. He can hardly change a light bulb. And you expect him to deal with IVs, catheters, bedpans, and fourteen different kinds of medication?"

"He killed his mother, Barry. The guy deserves to rot. You chop your mother with an axe in seven different places, you deserve to rot."

"This was a preventable homicide. Susan Allen should have

known better. She should have asked for home care right from the start."

But Marsh seemed not to hear.

"Point one, Barry. I want a suspect in the Latham case, and I want it fast. Point two, I want Wesley Rowe off the streets. We got to start making ourselves look good around here. I want him booked on first-degree, and I want you to forget about the social worker. I'll give you a few days to square it with the Park, but I want Rowe in here no later than Monday. Let's start acting like cops. We're not here to save the world, Barry. We're here to make arrests."

Gilbert smoldered for the next fifteen minutes. He stared at his blank computer screen, slouched in his chair, hands steepled before him, letting his anger flow through him. It filled all the crannies and backwaters of his subconscious, but after five minutes, the hot mist of its immediacy began to fade, and he was able to see through it. Wesley Rowe didn't deserve first-degree. Wesley Rowe was a forty-year-old child. Wesley Rowe needed help, but he didn't need, and certainly didn't deserve, twenty-five years in the Kingston Penitentiary. Still, Gilbert had to bring him in. Marsh gave the orders around here. But that didn't mean he was necessarily going to give Susan Allen a break.

He was just making a cup of instant coffee when John Jackson from Missing Persons entered the Homicide Office. Jackson was an older man, wore a three-piece suit, looked more like a lawyer than a Missing Persons detective. He said a few words to Sylvia Gideon, one of the secretaries. Sylvia turned around and pointed to Gilbert's desk. Jackson looked over the various work stations in the large central office and gave Gilbert a small wave. The Missing Persons detective weaved his way through the workstations to Gilbert's desk.

"You've got a hike to the cafeteria down here, don't you?" said Jackson.

Gilbert shrugged. "We don't eat much. We live on coffee."

Jackson nodded, deadpan. "I thought so." He held up a Xerox copy of something. "Thought you'd like to see this. You're working the Latham case, aren't you?"

"Joe and I."

"Her husband called this in."

Gilbert took the report. Dated the eighteenth of February, 9:07 A.M., the morning Cheryl was discovered at Dominion Malting.

"That doesn't make sense," he said. "You have to be gone at least forty-eight hours before you're considered missing. The security tape has her in the Glenarden the previous evening, less than twelve hours before. Why would he file a missing persons report?"

"I don't know," said Jackson. "That's why I thought you should see this. Is he trying to make himself look good?"

Gilbert glanced over the report again. "Maybe," he said. "Either that or he's just plain stupid." He put the report on his desk.

"Like pre-emptive cooperation," said Jackson.

"Yeah, exactly."

"Has he been notified?" asked Jackson.

Gilbert nodded. "We phoned yesterday. I'm going to see him today."

"Then I'll close it from our end, Barry," he said. Jackson gave him a grin that wasn't in the least bit envious. "You guys can have it."

Gilbert drove in an unmarked car to Latham's expensive three-storey home in Rosedale. The oaks were a hundred years old, thick behemoths that towered above the huge houses like dour guardians of wealth and prestige, leafless at this time of year, the stark tracery of their bare branches somehow unnerving against the pale grey sky. Latham's house had to be at least a century old as well, one of those late-Victorian brick-piles so prevalent in this part of Rosedale; yet its prim facade had been punctured with an assortment of thermal windows, one of them rising the full three storeys to the central gable. Skylights abounded. A glass sunroom had been added to the side.

Latham's Mercedes stood in the drive; Latham usually didn't leave for his office until noon. Not only a Mercedes, but a Chief Cherokee as well. Gilbert parked at the curb, walked up the drive, and checked the tires on both cars. Uniroyals on the Mercedes and Goodyears on the Cherokee. That by no means ruled Latham out. A Filipino man with a snow-blower emerged from the garage and approached him.

"Can I help you?" he asked.

"I'm Detective Gilbert," he said, pulling out his shield. "I'm here to see Mr. Latham."

The man pointed to the front door. "Go right up," he said. "Sally will see you in."

Gilbert climbed the steps to an elaborate porch made of brick, added to the original Victorian facade, somewhat out of character with the rest of the place, at least to Gilbert's mind. Latham was an architect. Let him play with his house. He was a partner in one of the largest architectural firms downtown. If he wanted to mix and match styles, that was his prerogative.

He knocked on the door. Sally answered. She, too, was Filipino, around thirty-five years old, with a cheery face, long black hair braided in a ponytail, wearing jeans, a sweatshirt, and an apron. Gilbert smelled coffee brewing within.

"Hi," she said. "Detective Gilbert, right? Come in. It's so cold out there. I'll let Mr. Latham know you're here."

"Thanks."

He gave his feet a wipe and followed her into a large front hall. Everything had been renovated. Everything had clean lines and well-defined angles, done in muted pastel shades. His eyes strayed over a large Chinese vase, a few abstract expressionist sculptures in white marble on pedestals, a Persian rug laid over the thick white broadloom. He followed Sally through an extensive pantry and entered the kitchen. The kitchen was bigger than his own living room. In the center stood an island with enough counter space to prepare a banquet; around the sides, endless cupboard space, two ranges, a microwave; and at the back a huge breakfast nook set against a capacious bay window which looked out onto a large terraced garden leading down to the steamy glass walls of an indoor swimming pool. Three pencil sketches hung on the wall, one neatly next to the other, each signed by Picasso; here was a man who could afford to hang Picassos in his kitchen.

"Have a chair," said Sally. Without asking, she brought him a cup of coffee and a Chelsea bun; the Chelsea bun itself looked like it cost ten dollars. "He's at his drafting table. I'll have to drag him away." She put her hands on her hips, making a face that was both scolding and indulgent. "This might take a minute."

He sat there trying not to feel overwhelmed. Every so often he would buy an *Architectural Digest*, a magazine that was really a home decorating manual for the excessively wealthy. And here he was, inside one of those homes. Was this what he had given up when he quit architectural school? The old regret came back. About the only architectural decision he had made in the last while was whether they were going to buy a pedestal sink or wall-mounted sink for the bathroom. Imagine if he had a space like this old house to work with. Nothing was so magical as light and space, and the uses humans put it to.

Charles Latham appeared at the kitchen doorway. Gilbert wasn't expecting someone so young. He was tall, not so much handsome as intelligent-looking, with unruly reddish hair receding from his prominent brow. He couldn't have been more than forty. He was stoop-shouldered, exceedingly thin, and wore prescription glasses, the kind that turned light or dark according to brightness, and his blue eyes behind the thick lenses looked somewhat small. He was pale, and the beige corduroy blazer with brown elbow patches seemed to accentuate his paleness. He looked like a man who had most probably had all sorts of respiratory problems as a child, thin-chested, scrawny, but mantis-like in his tallness; not a lady's man, no, definitely not, someone who was Joe Lombardo's antithesis, a man with no fashion sense—his brown slacks were two inches too short and he wore them high on his waist—a man with no flair. But a successful man. A man with a big house in Rosedale, a man who had married the petite and pretty Cheryl. A man who might have murdered Cheryl.

"Detective Gilbert," he said. "I'm sorry to have kept you waiting."

He looked emotionally frayed, done in by worry and exhaustion. Gilbert rose. "This is quite a place you have," he said.

"Thank you," he said. He poured a cup of coffee for himself. No sign of Sally anymore. "It's coming along." He slid into the chair opposite Gilbert; he seemed oblivious to the opulence of his surroundings.

"I'm sorry about your wife," said Gilbert.

Latham nodded, curling his lips tightly, his eyes fixed on the sugar bowl. "Anything I can do, detective," he said. "Anything at all."

Detective Gilbert took out his notebook and pen. "I understand the funeral's tomorrow. Over in Mount Pleasant."

"Yes," said Latham. "Tom's arranged most of it. I'm still in a million pieces. I can hardly . . ."

Gilbert studied Latham. If it was an act, it was a good one. He seemed genuinely ripped apart by the death of his wife; not that this in itself proved his innocence, especially if he had killed her out of passion. Yet the crime itself didn't have the mark of passion; and in that sense, Latham's apparent grief played in his favor. Gently, gently, he told himself.

"I understand you and your wife separated last year," he said. "By the way, this is excellent coffee."

Latham gestured absently at the kitchen doorway. "Sally gets it somewhere."

"Have you always had . . . hired help?"

"I'm not much of a cook. Any extra time I scrape from the office I spend in my garden."

"Do you have any children?"

"Not yet," he said. "Some day, maybe. I was hoping that Cheryl and I might reconciliate . . . that we would eventually go on and . . . Sally and Danny are great. I come home and . . . I don't know, I trust them, they like me, not because I employ them, just because . . . we understand each other. I don't know why Cheryl couldn't get along with them."

Gilbert raised his eyebrows. "Cheryl didn't like them?"

"It's not that she didn't like them, it's just that she thought she could run the place by herself." He rubbed his long-fingered hands together, put his elbows on the table and leaned forward. "Do you have any specific questions, detective? Or any ideas how I can help you in a substantive way?"

"Mr. Latham, we're still just feeling our way around this right now."

"Please, call me Charles."

"I'm just trying to get to know Cheryl. I find that helps. You say she thought she could run this place by herself."

Latham glanced out the window, where a sparrow landed on top of the bird feeder.

"She was nervous about strangers. She considered Sally and Danny strangers. She wouldn't make an effort to get to know them. I won't say we had a perfect marriage, detective. Of course I was willing to make some changes. I knew I would have to make some changes. Marriage is all about change. But I also expected compromise. Cheryl had to have things a particular way. If she couldn't have things her way, she either got anxious or upset. Things always had to be exact with Cheryl." Gilbert thought of the glasses lined up in even rows in the glass cupboard at the Glenarden. "I knew she was a fastidious woman when I first met her. That didn't bother me. I thought it was a plus. I'm a fastidious man. When she first moved in three years ago, everything was fine. But then she slowly tried to take over."

"And where did you meet her?"

"At a fund-raiser for her father."

"You filed a missing persons report yesterday morning." Gilbert took a sip of his coffee and looked out the window; somewhere on the grounds he heard the high thin buzz of Danny using the snow-blower. "To tell you the truth, we find that odd, Mr. Latham. On the security tape, she enters the Glenarden at 9:16 Tuesday night. You call twelve hours later. By definition she has to be gone at least forty-eight hours before she can be considered missing. Obviously you knew something was up. Obviously you expected her to be there Wednesday morning, and when she wasn't, you called."

Latham nodded. He got up from the table and walked over to the wall phone. Sitting on a small shelf beneath the phone was a sleek black answering machine.

"I want you to listen to this, detective. I got home around eleven o'clock Tuesday night, and this is what I found on my answering machine."

He pressed the play button, the tape rewound, and Latham pressed the search button until he came to the appropriate message.

"This is Cheryl," said Latham.

The tape hummed, and Cheryl spoke. "Hi, Charles." She spoke in a low voice. The tension cut through. "I'm in a bit of a jam right now. Do you think you could come over? Right away? Or whenever you hear this message? There's someone here who . . . I don't know, I think I'm going to need a lawyer, and I thought—"

But then the message ended; no indication of violence, just a sudden cut-off. Gilbert remembered the phone in the waste-paper basket. But there was something that didn't jibe with this tape, something that left him unconvinced.

"Is that her bird in the background? The parrot?"

"That's him," said Latham. "He's a squawker."

Gilbert stared at Latham. The bird was dead. True, there remained the possibility that this message came before the bird was killed. But there was also the possibility that this tape was perhaps months or weeks or even a year old, that Latham had saved it on purpose to use as a decoy when it came time to murder his wife.

"Do you mind if I take that tape?" he asked

Latham opened the cover, snapped out the tape, and gave it to Gilbert. "It's yours."

Gilbert squirreled it away in his accordion-style briefcase.

"So you called Missing Persons because you got this message from her the previous night." Gilbert cocked his head. "Gee, Charles, I don't get it. She sounds like she's in legal trouble. Nothing to file a missing persons report about. Did you actually go over once you got home on Tuesday night?"

Latham nodded. "As fast as I could." He sat down in his chair, lifted his cup of coffee halfway to his lips, but then put it back on the table. "You see, Detective Gilbert, this separation wasn't my idea. I love Cheryl. I'll do anything for her. Do you know that old Cole Porter song, *Night and Day*? That's what it was like for me when Cheryl came along." He lifted his coffee again and this time managed to take a sip. He nodded at Gilbert's briefcase. "That message, she asked me to come over, I was hoping for a reconciliation, so of course I went over."

"So you arrived at the Glenarden at approximately what time?"

Latham's brow furrowed. "A little after midnight."

"Do you have a key?"

"Not to her apartment. But she gave me one to her building."

Gilbert remembered the security tape. "What were you wearing?"

"My parka."

Four men, all in parkas, all unidentified because of deep hoods.

"I can't help noticing you have a big bandage on your hand," said Gilbert.

Latham looked at the thick gauze bandage. "I'm an absolute idiot in the kitchen," he said. "Thank God I have Sally."

"So you got in the building and you went upstairs. You went upstairs and you knocked on Cheryl's door. Did anyone see you?"

"No. The halls were empty."

"And earlier in the evening you were at work."

"Correct."

"And did anybody see you there?"

Latham frowned. "I'm not a suspect, am I, detective?"

"Nobody said you were. But we have routine questions we like to ask. So we can narrow the field. What time did you get to work on Monday night?"

"Around nine-thirty. I had a few things to pick up."

"So if I were to ask the security guard—"

"I went in through the underground parking lot. You have to have a special access card. No one saw me."

"And what about when you got up to the office? It's a big firm, isn't it? Someone must have been working late."

Latham's face grew stony. "No," he said, "no one was there."

"Okay, okay," said Gilbert. "Don't look so worried. You just tell me what happened. You got home at eleven, you listened to Cheryl's message, and you rushed over to the Glenarden. You used your key to gain access, you went upstairs and knocked on her door." Gilbert raised his eyebrows. "Then what happened?"

"She didn't answer. I couldn't hear a thing inside. Not even that damn parrot of hers."

Gilbert contemplated Latham; maybe he was telling the truth, maybe not.

"So then what did you do?"

Latham shrugged. "I went home."

"And in the morning you called Missing Persons. That's the part I don't get."

Latham took a deep breath, pushed his chair away from the table and crossed his legs. "Maybe I should explain a little bit about what happened between Cheryl and I over the last year. So you can better understand my emotional state on Tuesday morning. I know it's not a logical thing. Phoning Missing Persons. I can see it bugs you. But I've been keyed up for a year."

"Then tell me about your year."

Latham glanced toward the kitchen door, collecting his thoughts. "I don't know how things could have so badly deteriorated between Cheryl and I," he said. "It wasn't any one thing in particular, just a lot of small things. For two years we were fine. But then we began to fight. Are you married, detective?"

Gilbert nodded.

"Then you know how married couples argue. They argue for the sake of arguing. They argue because they haven't had enough sleep, or because they're feeling cranky, or because they're hungry. Sometimes it's about money. Sometimes it's about other things. Cheryl was always independent about money. She kept her job even after we got married. We argued over just about damn near everything.

"We bought a painting, a Louis d'Niberville, a mother toweling a child dry at the seaside, perfect, I thought, for the hallway leading to the indoor swimming pool. She insisted we hang it in the old sewing room. I don't know why. There's hardly any wall space in that room. And it's a big painting, something you have to stand back from to truly appreciate. Isn't that silly? That was our first big argument. I let her have her way. Why not? I saw that it was upsetting her. I knew she had to have things just so. She got panicky otherwise. Like if she couldn't control the world the world would somehow control her."

Gilbert remained quiet. Somewhere off in the house he heard a clock softly chiming. The coffeemaker made a sudden bubbly sound, hissed once or twice, then lapsed into silence.

"Then we began having arguments about Danny and Sally," continued Latham. "It's not that she didn't trust them. Danny and Sally are the most trustworthy people in the world. Cheryl was just a private person. I've always had live-in help. My parents had live-in help. It's never bothered me. But Cheryl felt as if she were being scrutinized all the time. Sally's the best housekeeper I've ever had. Everything's always spotless. And her cooking's great. But Cheryl began to hover

over Sally. Cheryl could never relax when Sally was around. I don't know why. Sally's easygoing. Sally will forgive a lot. But finally Sally asked me to talk to Cheryl. Cheryl and I argued." Latham smiled in self-deprecation. "I'm probably giving you the impression that we argued all the time. But we didn't. Most of the time, things were great. We were like two high school kids. We couldn't keep our hands off each other. We really loved each other. But then we would have these fights. I didn't want to fight. I wanted to accommodate her as far as I could. She really wanted to be mistress of her own household, I guess that's what it was. So I finally let Sally and Danny go. I gave them glowing references. They both got jobs immediately. I had to beg them to come back when Cheryl finally left me. I also had to give them a whopping increase in pay, but I don't care, they're worth it."

A black squirrel climbed the bird feeder, scaring the sparrow away.

"So you resented this?" suggested Gilbert. "You felt like you betrayed Sally and Danny?"

"I felt . . . not exactly as if I'd betrayed them, but . . . I just felt sad that we would find ourselves in a situation where I would have to ask them to leave. And whether I resented it . . . well, yes, I suppose I did. I appreciate order, detective. I like a clean house. I can work better when I know everything's in order. A lot of people are like that. But Cheryl carried it to extremes."

Gilbert wondered what this had to do with phoning Missing Persons, but let Latham continue. It was as if Latham had never been able to talk to anybody about this; as a veteran of thousands of interviews and interrogations, Gilbert recognized the syndrome well; Latham was ventilating. Sometimes a detective learned more this way than from a direct question.

"Not so much resentment, but more a mounting frustration," said Latham. He tapped the kitchen table a few times.

"Then . . . I don't know . . . I guess it was a month or two before our separation, she started asking me for money. This was new. She'd never asked me for cash outright. And I gave it to her. It wasn't the money that bothered me." He gestured at the house. "I've got more than I can use . . . I just wanted to know what she needed it for. What's so strange about that? She didn't want to tell me. It became an issue of trust for her. She was my wife, if she needed money, I should give it to her, what's mine was hers, etcetera, and I should be able to trust her. After all, I trusted her with everything else."

"How much money?" asked Gilbert.

Latham gave him a vague shrug. "I didn't keep track." He squinted, pushed his glasses up his nose. "It must have been five or six thousand."

"And this happened about a year ago last Christmas?"

"About that."

"Do you think it had anything to do with Christmas?" asked Gilbert. "Maybe she had to buy Christmas presents or something."

Latham shook his head lackadaisically. "I have no idea," he said. "By that time I didn't care. I just wanted to keep her happy." Out in the yard, Danny appeared from behind the indoor swimming pool, pushing the snow-blower before him, sending a cloud of snow into the air. "Then, in January, things really took a turn for the worse. She started looking for fights. Like she wanted to find an excuse to leave me." He tapped the table. "She wanted to move this table. I had this nook specifically built so I could put a table here. This is my favorite spot in the whole house. I wanted to eat my breakfast here and look at my garden. She was cooking bacon with a spatula over by the island there. I felt like I'd been tackled when she told me we had to move the table. I'd given into her every other wish. I lost my temper. I hardly ever lose my temper. The fight really wasn't about the table. It was about everything else, about all the small changes I'd been forced to make, about Sally and Danny, everything. My garden's special to me, Detective Gilbert. There's nothing I enjoy more than sitting at this window and looking at my garden. I had a furniture-maker make this table specifically for this nook."

"So you said no," said Gilbert.

Latham gave him a rough defiant nod. "That's right. I said no. And we fought. We argued. And she had that spatula covered with molten grease in her hand. And she always moves her hands a lot when she argues. But I honestly think, even to this day, that she flung that grease at me on purpose." He pointed to two whitish spots on his cheek. "You can still see the scars. And . . . I don't know . . . I lashed out. It was more reflex. When something physically hurts you like that—and let me tell you, detective, that grease hurt like hell—you instinctively . . ." Latham fumbled for words.

"You hit her?" asked Gilbert.

Latham's defiance disappeared like air out of a balloon. He looked suddenly overcome with guilt. "I didn't mean to," he said. "I never hit anyone in my life. And to hit my wife . . . I don't know how it happened. Like the pressure built up, and the grease just set it free, and I didn't really hit her that hard, just gave her a kind of a light cuff across the top of the head, it didn't do much more than mess up her hair. But as far as Cheryl was concerned, that was it. I'd crossed a line. I begged her. I pleaded with her. I dragged the table away from the nook right there and then, but she kept on screaming at me. She flipped. I'd never seen her like that. From then on, I was completely despicable to Cheryl." Latham leaned forward and stared at the detective intently. "I'm only human, detective. I lost my temper. It's the first and only time I've ever lashed out at anyone. I told her it would never happen again. But as far as she was concerned, I didn't exist anymore. At least not as her husband. One lapse, Detective Gilbert, that's all it took.

One isolated incident. You think she would be able to forgive me. I'm not perfect. But you think she would have given me a second chance. It was just a light tap. It didn't even hurt. And it was completely out of character for me. She knew I would never do it again."

Gilbert stared at Latham; and he recalled Blackstein's autopsy report. All the distant fractures, the missing teeth, the scarred spleen. Beaten badly as a child. Under those circumstances, was Cheryl's reaction so bizarre? He wondered if Latham knew. Probably not. Child-abuse victims usually buried things. And this didn't sound too good for Latham from a suspect standpoint. He'd already placed himself at the Glenarden on the night of the murder. Now he was explaining to Gilbert how unfairly, how cruelly he had been treated by his wife. He had a cut on his hand and they had unidentified blood in the kitchen sink. He had no provable alibi. Plus no forced entry at the Glenarden, which meant Cheryl knew her killer.

"And that's when she left you?" said Gilbert.

Latham nodded morosely. "The very next day. She stayed with a friend from work at first. I grew obsessed with knowing where she was. I still am. That's what you have to understand about Tuesday. I always have to know where she is. When she left me, Dorothy was dead and Cheryl didn't want to impose on Tom. The following month she moved into the Glenarden. Of course I tried desperately to win her back."

"But she refused to see you."

"At first she did. But after a month or two, we started seeing each other for coffee occasionally. She helped me with some business now and again. There's a Starbucks up there. I didn't press her immediately. I felt I had to give it the velvet glove. If I could show her that I was really a nice man, that I was truly sorry, even remorseful for clipping her on the head like that, I thought she might take me back. In May she helped me plant the annuals. I thought things were going well. But then she started asking me for money again." Latham paused. "Five hundred dollars. Sometimes a thousand. I was only too happy to give it to her. I didn't even ask her what she wanted it for. I really didn't care. I thought I was making headway. I was always phoning her, always dropping in at her work. I just wanted to know where she was." He shook his head, and he looked ripped apart again, and guilty as could be. "That's what happened Tuesday morning. I guess I panicked. I phoned and phoned. I was worried about the message she'd left. She wasn't at home and she wasn't at work. I thought something might have happened to her. I started thinking about the money. I had to know where she was. My old habit. I simply had to know that. I didn't intentionally phone Missing Persons but that's who they put me through to." He shrugged. "I wanted to find her. I wanted to make sure she was safe. And I was willing to try anything." He looked at Gilbert quizzically. "Is there anything so strange about that?"

Chapter Six

Gilbert arrived at Mount Joseph General Hospital a little after one that same afternoon. A hundred hospital workers—nurses, technicians, housekeeping staff—marched with pickets in front of the admitting drive-through, not a strike, just a one-day protest, with many of the placards featuring Tom Webb's name; the hospitals faced the same eighteen-percent cut. He parked the car, grabbed his briefcase, and entered the hospital, his mind still half on the things Charles Latham had told him this morning.

The hospital, built in the 1950s, was a study in institutional gloom; dour portraits of past presidents hung one after the other in the lobby, the wood panelling had faded to the color of potato skins, and the small lights hanging from the ceiling did little but cast anemic pools of light into the general dimness. He turned left past the volunteer office and continued down the hall. Glass cabinets displayed the handicrafts of rehab-therapy patients; there was nothing handy or crafty about these small paintings and clay sculptures; they were malformed, accidental, and spoke of the tragedy of mangled bodies trying to rebuild themselves.

He passed the Urology Department and finally came to the Social Work Department. He entered a small reception area. The receptionist, a fragile-looking woman with wispy black hair pulled into a severe bun, peered up from her computer.

"Yes?" she said.

Gilbert pulled out his shield. "I'm Detective Barry Gilbert," he said. "I have an appointment to see Susan Allen."

The receptionist looked at Gilbert with a perplexed frown, then buzzed Susan Allen's office, lifting the receiver to her ear. "You have a Detective Barry Gilbert to see you," she said.

The receptionist listened to Susan Allen's reply, put the receiver down, then looked up at Gilbert.

"She'll be out in a minute," she said. "You can have a seat over there."

"Thanks."

Gilbert sat down. He stared at the receptionist, trying to figure her out. Before he could ponder further, Susan Allen's door opened and a man, his face red, his eyes set in barely suppressed fury, well-dressed in a suit and tie, marched from the office, and, without looking once to the left or right, or even so much as acknowledging the beleaguered receptionist, left the Social Work office and disappeared down the hall.

Susan Allen appeared at her door. She stared after the man, her face strained, obviously upset about the encounter, and turned to the receptionist.

"Liz," she said. "Liz, he's usually not like this . . . he usually . . ."

Liz stared at Susan forlornly. "Did you get it settled?" she asked.

Susan turned around, seeming to see Detective Gilbert for the first time. She looked at Gilbert as if she didn't know who

he was. Then her memory jogged. "Detective . . ." She struggled to remember his name.

Gilbert rose, extended his hand. "Gilbert," he said. "Barry
Gilbert. I came to talk to you about Wesley Rowe."

"Oh!" she said, as if she'd been jabbed by a pin.

Gilbert glanced toward the door. "But I see I came at a bad
time." He let his hand fall to his side. "If you want me to
come back some other—"

"No," she said. She looked at the door again. "No, not at
all, I'm sorry, I . . ." She forced a smile. "Come this way."
She tried to shoehorn some enthusiasm into her voice, putting
it on for Liz's sake. "Please," she said. "Liz, hold my calls
until we're done."

He followed the social worker into her office. She was a
tall woman, about forty-five, wore a light brown blazer with
padded shoulders and a matching skirt, had a slim build, too
slim, as if she had a problem. She looked harried. Her eyes
narrowed, and she concentrated on Gilbert, her silvery irises
squeezing against her pupils.

"I thought we had this cleared up," she said, her voice now
devoid of enthusiasm. Her voice was hard, flat, demanding.
"Someone else was here yesterday to pick up the records."

Gilbert opened his briefcase and pulled out the badly typed
social work report on Wesley Rowe; then he pulled out a
sample social work report from Marion Rowe's chart, one
typed by a transcriptionist in Medical Records and printed on
the Lasotec.

"That's what I want to talk about," he said. "I'm just wondering about the difference in these reports. I was wondering
why one was done on a laser printer while the other was done
on some kind of typewriter."

She stared at the reports; and she became so still Gilbert
thought she was never going to move again. Gilbert hated

this. He hated making Susan Allen squirm like this. She wasn't a criminal. But because of her negligence, or maybe because she was overworked, Wesley Rowe was up on a first-degree murder charge.

"Look, give me a break, will you?" she said.

Gilbert stared at her. He held the stare for close to ten seconds as he watched her hands come together, her head bow, her streaky blonde hair fall over her face; she picked at the nail polish on one of her nails. Quietly, he put the reports back in his briefcase.

"Susan, Wesley Rowe's going to be arrested for first-degree murder on Monday," he said.

She stopped picking at her nail polish; she kept her head bowed but he knew she was listening.

"You know what he's like," continued Gilbert. "He's got the mental aptitude of a nine-year-old. You shouldn't have rubber-stamped him as his mother's primary caregiver."

"He seemed perfectly fine to me."

"Susan, he's lived with his mother his whole life. He can hardly look after himself let alone a sick mother with bladder cancer. I've read the chart. First the bladder, then the lungs, and finally into the liver. Here's a man-child who can barely spell his own name, and he's faced with watching his own mother die, not to mention suffer, and he's expected to ease her suffering." Gilbert shook his head. "Well, he eased her suffering all right. In the only way he knew how."

"What do you want me to do?" said Susan. Her voice was thick. But Gilbert wasn't about to stop.

"How many times did you meet with them? How carefully did you assess the situation?"

"We have a form. I filled out the form."

"I checked the chart. You met with them five times. The staff doctor indicated palliative care."

"Wesley said he wanted to look after his mother at home."

"He's incapable of making decisions for himself." Gilbert shook his head. "Let me see if I've got this right. The doctor doesn't assess the patient's social situation, he assesses only their medical condition. It's up to the Social Work Department to deal with the social issues facing a patient, including the family situation, especially in regard to palliative care. Should you not have drawn up placement papers for Marion Rowe? Should she not have been placed in a palliative care institution? Was it really the proper decision to leave her at home with Wesley?"

"At the time, it seemed like the best decision."

"You typed this report and stuck an old date on it afterward. To cover your tracks. It's obvious. I don't know how you thought you could get away with it. I'm not blaming you. We all make mistakes. But now we have to figure out what we're going to do about it."

Susan Allen stared at him. The corners of her lips tightened, drawing into an unintentional pout. Her eyes grew misty. She looked quickly away, sniffled, as if she had a cold. Her mouth opened, like she was about to say something, but then she shut it, as if she knew no matter how many explanations she came up with, none could be satisfactory, none could ever bring Marion Rowe back, or entirely spare Wesley Rowe the consequences of his actions. She finally sat back, pressing her shoulders deep into the worn upholstery of her office chair, and stared at him, the hard edge coming back to her eyes.

"The Marion Rowe file was dumped on me with fifty others," she said. "We lost two staff in here this December, and the rest of us had to take up the slack. Cutbacks." Her brow creased in silent appeal. "We work twelve-hour days around here," she said. "We get paid for eight. We work the free overtime because we're afraid we'll lose our jobs if we don't. Wesley seemed a little rough, but nothing marked him as overtly handicapped. So I filled out the form. I saved myself the placement report." She took a deep breath. "If this case gets to the College of Physicians for review, I'm history."

She sat back and put her palms flat on her desk.

"And what if Wesley Rowe goes to prison for first-degree murder?"

She shrugged. "He killed her, didn't he?" She gestured toward the chart. "I've read the coroner's report. He axed her seven times. The first officer at the scene found the axe embedded in her head. That seems like murder to me."

"Ms. Allen, you don't seem to understand. What I'm asking is simple. Appear as a witness at Wesley Rowe's murder trial. Tell the judge what happened. It's going to affect the sentencing."

She again seemed to freeze. Her eyes took on a stark quality.

"The RMT would have me out the door the next day," she said.

"I'm just asking for help. Wesley doesn't deserve this."

She looked angry. "And I don't deserve to lose my job."

"I don't want to force your hand, Ms. Allen," he said. "I want you to do it willingly."

Gilbert held her gaze; the mist in her eyes thickened. She yanked a tissue from the box and dabbed her lower lids. A hard one, this. She was right. She was probably going to lose her job.

"You're really going to do this, aren't you?" she said.

"I'm sorry, Ms. Allen. But I'm not going to see Wesley Rowe go to jail for twenty-five years when I know for a fact this homicide should have never happened in the first place."

As he left the Mount Joseph General Hospital, he saw the evening edition of the *Toronto Star* inside the vending box beside the revolving door. He read the half-inch headline. CABINET MINISTER'S STEPDAUGHTER FOUND SLAIN.

Ronald Roffey had the byline. Gilbert didn't bother to read the details. As far as he was concerned, there were no details. No details, just a lot of pressure, thanks to Roffey.

Five o'clock that evening Gilbert and Lombardo met Sonia Bailey, Cheryl's neighbor, at the Glenarden.

As the three of them walked down the hall together toward Cheryl's apartment, Lombardo eyed the lovely mulatto woman surreptitiously. Sonia had about six inches on Joe, but that wasn't going to stop Lombardo; it never did. Gilbert gave him a look, but Lombardo ignored the older detective.

A crime-scene notice had been pasted on Cheryl's door and an X of yellow crime-scene tape had been tacked to the door frame. Gilbert untacked the tape, took out the key, and opened the door. The three of them entered the apartment. Gilbert turned on the light.

"The pictures have been taken down," he said, "and you can see that someone's looked through all those books over there. Just ignore that. Just tell us if you think anything's been moved around."

Sonia nodded and looked around the apartment. Her eyes were wide in mild distress; she could feel the ghosts in here, but she was doing her best to ignore them.

"Everything looks the same," she said. "Nothing's been changed."

She scanned the room again and gave Gilbert a shrug. To-day she wore bright red lipstick; her lips, in her coppery face, looked like a piece of tropical fruit, had the blush of an over-ripe mango.

"Let's go to the kitchen," said Gilbert.

The three went into the kitchen. Sonia glanced around.

She shrugged. "Everything's the same," she said.

They went to the bedroom, then the bathroom. "Nothing's been changed," said Sonia.

So they went back to the living room.

"We're sorry to inconvenience you like this, Ms. Bailey," said Lombardo. "We just thought that on the off chance . . . before we turn the apartment over to Mr. Waxman . . ."

She turned to Lombardo; she smiled, the way all women smiled at Joe. "I wish I could have helped you . . . more . . ."

Gilbert watched the two younger people; their eyes held. Lombardo was good with his eyes. He could convey the most complicated emotions with his eyes, just as he could send the most overt signals with them. Before Gilbert could stop him, Lombardo handed his card to Sonia.

"Here's my card," he said. "You call me if you remember anything, or if you have any concerns."

Her eyes widened. She glanced at Gilbert. She already had Gilbert's card. Gilbert kept his mouth shut.

Lombardo gestured at the room, never for a second losing his charm. "Maybe you can take one last look for us," he said.

So she scanned the living room again. Then she looked at the floor. And her eyes narrowed.

"Actually . . ." A pretty but puzzled frown came to her face. She looked first at Lombardo, then at Gilbert, then back to Lombardo. Then she looked at the floor again. The two detectives stared at Sonia. "The rug," she said. The two detectives looked down at the rug. "She usually has that corner facing the window." Rectangle room, a rectangle rug, but with the rug angled, an interior design tactic to create the illusion of space. "Now it's pointing to the bookcase," she said.

Gilbert knelt and had a closer look at the rug. "Are you sure?" he asked.

She nodded. "She always had that corner pointing to the window."

Gilbert clutched the corner of the rug and lifted; on the floor underneath he saw two paint chips, each pale green; none of the rooms in Cheryl's apartment were pale green. Also, on the underweave, he saw a large grease smudge. He carefully lifted the paint chip and showed it to Cheryl.

"Do you have paint like this anywhere in the building?" he asked.

She peered at the paint. "That's from the laundry room," she said. "The laundry room is green."

"Those come from the laundry room?" he said.

"Yes."

"Where's the laundry room?"

"It's downstairs," she said. "I'll show you."

They left Cheryl's apartment and went downstairs to the laundry room. Nestled at the back in the building's half-basement, the laundry room had large netted glass windows facing the rear drive and the tenant garages. Each of the windows opened on a center transom, so that as the bottom half was pulled in, the top half was levered out. The transom was well greased; he thought of the grease on the rug. The paint on the window frame, pale green, flaked, revealing an older beige underneath. Gilbert glanced around for security cameras but he saw none.

"There's no key?" he said to Sonia. "You don't need a key to get in?"

She shook her head. "No," she said.

Lombardo opened one of the windows; it swung easily. And the gap was wide enough to shove a rolled up rug through; even a rug with a body in it. Lombardo took out a glassine bag, put paint chips inside, then used a cotton swab to wipe some of the grease up. He looked at Gilbert.

"Ten to one we get a match," he said.

*   *   *

After leaving the Glenarden they drove back to College Street in silence. Gilbert kept glancing at Lombardo. Finally, it became too much for Lombardo.

"What's wrong?" he asked Gilbert. "Why do you keep looking at me like that? You should keep your eyes on the road."

Gilbert didn't reply, continued to drive, sticking to the right of the road at a stodgy sixty kilometers per hour. How could he put this to Joe so he didn't take it the wrong way?

"So you liked Sonia," he said at last.

"Is that what this is about?" Lombardo sighed.

"Joe, I think you have to be careful."

"I gave her my card. Is that a crime?"

"You know what I'm talking about."

Lombardo looked out the window, where the snow fell in thick and steady flakes.

"She's pretty," he said.

"I know she's pretty," said Gilbert. They bumped over the streetcar tracks at St. Clair Avenue. "But you've got to be careful. Marsh is watching you. You can't be trying to pick up every witness you see. Marsh is just looking for an excuse. And I'd hate to see you give him one."

Lombardo grew solemn, stared pensively at the glove compartment. The snow didn't look as if it were going to quit any time soon and Gilbert decreased his speed to forty kilometers per hour as he eased the Lumina down the Avenue Road hill toward Davenport.

"Did you see the way she looked at me?" said Lombardo.

Gilbert nodded, checked his rearview mirror. "I saw," he said.

Lombardo gave his head a slow melancholy shake. "I don't know, Barry. I have a feeling about her."

"You always have a feeling, Joe."

"No, this time I'm serious."

"You're always serious, Joe."

They parked on Mount Pleasant Road the next day, just south of Eglinton Avenue, across from the Hennessey-Newbigging Funeral Home. The streets were clogged with snow and it was still coming down. Gilbert sipped his coffee and looked at Lombardo. The funeral service for Cheryl Latham was still going on inside and wouldn't be over for another few minutes. They had two detectives inside, and another two at the burial plot. They had both video and camera surveillance. Lombardo was having a hard time concentrating. Lombardo had spent an hour with Marsh this morning.

"Did you remind him of the Sharon Brierley collar?" asked Gilbert.

"I gave him everything," said Lombardo. "I pulled out every star case I'd ever had. You know what he said about the Brierley case?"

"What?"

"He said I took too long. What's he expect with arson? His idea of a perp is a guy who's still holding a gun and has blood all over his pants. I had to build that case. I had to go back. I had to search. I don't bluster my way through interrogations the way he does. I go armed to the teeth with evidence. Does he think evidence grows on trees in an arson-murder case?"

Gilbert saw movement at the side entrance of the funeral home. Six pallbearers carried out Cheryl's coffin at hip level. They slid it into the back of the hearse. Mourners emerged from the front door, walked around to the small parking lot, and started getting into the cars for the drive to Mount Pleasant Cemetery.

"Look," said Gilbert, pointing. "There's Webb."

But Lombardo seemed oblivious.

"I told him you can't rush these things," he said. "You saw what was left of that apartment. Nothing. The only thing we had was some accelerant patterns and a corpse charred beyond recognition."

Gilbert shrugged, determined to make Lombardo feel better.

"Don't worry about it," he said. "Marsh doesn't like it when anybody has to leave rotation for more than a week. It offends his sense of order."

"We had the whole city clamoring about that kid. If I hadn't left rotation, she'd still be open, and Ling would be breathing down Marsh's back."

"What about the Byrnes case?"

"Same thing. He didn't like how extensive it was. He thinks we should all get our collars within two days of the crime, a week at the most. He thinks he's still in patrol."

"That's Latham over there," said Gilbert. "The tall man with the glasses?" He pointed.

Latham had tears in his eyes. Lombardo was actually able to get his mind off Marsh long enough so he could look at Latham.

"He needs a better tailor," was all Lombardo had to say about Latham.

Sally, the Filipino housekeeper, led Latham down the freshly salted steps, holding his elbow, directing him the way she might direct an old man. Gilbert's eyes strayed to the parking lot. Danny waited by the Mercedes. The theory so far was that Cheryl knew her killer. He took out his notebook and scribbled an entry. Cheryl knew Sally and Danny. And it hadn't been a particularly amicable relationship.

"He's got a two-minute memory," said Lombardo, going back to Marsh. "He doesn't remember the DeMarco collar or the Bush collar. Those were tough cases. Has he ever done an exhumation?"

"No," said Gilbert.

"Then how would he know?" he said. "He has no idea how hard I worked on the Bush case, how I had to go back ten years and find that forged signature. He's not interested. He said learn your ABCs, Joe: arrest, book, convict. Like it's really that simple. I'm telling you, Barry, he's got his sights set on me. When the cuts come, I'm going to be one of the first to go."

Lombardo smacked the dashboard with the palm of his hand.

Tom Webb got into the lead limousine while Sally helped Latham into the back seat of his Mercedes.

"Just forget it, Joe," said Gilbert. "There's nothing you can do."

"I'm going to fight it if he picks me," he said. "I'm not going back to patrol."

"I liked patrol," said Gilbert.

"Oh, Christ, you're not going to tell me another Alvin Matchett story are you?"

"He was a good cop, Joe."

"I'm serious, Barry, I was meant for this work. I'll take it right to Ling if I have to."

"Relax, Joe," said Gilbert. "You're not going back to patrol. Once we find Cheryl's killer, they'll keep you in Homicide forever. You'll have cobwebs all over you by the time they let you out."

"So I guess we find him."

"If it means your job," said Gilbert.

"Which I think it does," said Lombardo.

They followed the funeral procession down the slope toward Davisville, crossed Davisville, then climbed the short incline, where the asphalt in the road had been worn bare to reveal fifty-year-old paving bricks and long forgotten street-car tracks. Hundreds of gravestones, each heaped with a thick layer of snow, stood rank upon rank on either side of the road beyond the wrought iron fence. The Mount Pleasant Cemetery was the biggest, oldest, and most prestigious cemetery in the city. Not that the dead cared much about prestige.

Up ahead, the escort cop, with his Harley-and-sidecar, his white helmet and jodhpurs, his reflective sunglasses and motorcycle boots, sat casually at the gate, watching the cars file in. Gilbert followed the procession into the cemetery.

The cemetery roadway curved and twisted through hummocks and dales; trees of every variety sprang up from the desolate snowscape: dogwoods, cedars, aspens, poplars, ash, beech, spruce, pine, oak, and a half dozen species of maple. The cars up ahead slowed and Gilbert saw the grave site. He veered away from the procession, down a side road, and drove up a small incline. At the top, a mausoleum, made out of red granite, sat like a miniature castle among a grove of birch trees. Snow fell gently from the grey sky.

They got out and trudged through the snow until they stood in front of the mausoleum. In the dale below, people left their cars and gathered around the grave site. The minister held the order of service before him, waiting. Once everyone was gathered, the minister began with a prayer, but the words were too faint for Gilbert to hear. The twenty-five mourners kept their heads bowed.

Gilbert lifted his binoculars and looked at Webb; one of his people held a black umbrella above his head. Webb's face was expressionless. Gilbert moved on to Latham. Latham looked grey. Then on to Sally. Nothing untoward or disrespectful in her face. Then on to some of the other mourners. There was Shirley Chan, the Chinese girl Sonia had spoken of; they would get to her soon. And there was Bev Campbell, Cheryl's exercise instructor. There were three blind people in the crowd, people from the Canadian National Institute for the Blind, where Cheryl worked as a senior coordinator. And then there was . . . a tall man . . . did he recognize this man? . . . standing at the back . . . something so familiar about this man . . . by the sycamore tree . . . could it be? Gilbert adjusted the focus of his binoculars. It had to be. The man was obviously here in an official capacity, was wired for communications with an earphone in his left ear . . . security for Thomas Webb? The man scanned the crowd cautiously, looking through dark sunglasses. He had close-cropped sandy hair . . . good God, it couldn't be . . . Gilbert felt himself smiling . . . because now he knew it had to be . . . it could be no other.

Alvin Matchett, still as trim as ever after all these years, after all that trouble, as cool as ice, scanning the crowd, the surrounding tombstones, looking for trouble, always on top of it . . .

"Barry?" said Lombardo.

"Speak of the devil," said Gilbert. He took the binoculars from his eyes. "See that tall man over there?" he asked. "The security guy?"

Lombardo lifted his own binoculars. "Yeah?" he said.

"That's my old partner," said Gilbert, his smile now feeling stitched in place. "From patrol. That's Alvin Matchett."

At the wake an hour later, held in the main reception room of the Hennessey-Newbigging Funeral Home, Barry Gilbert and Alvin Matchett got a chance to catch up with each other.

Gilbert learned that after the Dennison shooting, Matchett signed on with the Ontario Provincial Police, first as a constable up north at their Red Lake Detachment, then as a detective in their financial crimes section. He was then offered a job as Sergeant with Legislative Security at the Provincial Parliament Buildings.

"I was assigned to Webb," said Matchett. "I started doing little extras for him. He finally offered me a job on his own staff at a lot more money. I couldn't refuse. I guess I'm his Man Friday. He can't do without me."

Gilbert scanned the reception room. Latham stood over in the corner looking out of place, awkward, as the various guests came and went. A buffet table was set up with sandwiches, coffee, tea, punch, and a fruit and cheese platter. People formed knots, talked to each other, the blind people as still as statues, unsure of their surroundings, the sighted people occasionally leading them to the buffet table, or to the washroom, or to Charles Latham.

"I thought you still might come to our baseball games," said Gilbert.

Matchett shrugged. "I was up in Red Lake all that time. And when I came back . . ." He shook his head. "It just didn't feel right."

"But you were cleared," said Gilbert.

"I was cleared, but I still didn't want to . . . I just thought it best if I made a clean break. Going to games . . . I didn't want to open old wounds. I know you guys went into a serious losing streak after I left, but I . . ." He grinned, trying to keep a light tone.

Gilbert shook his head. "No one understood about Laraby," he said.

"I know."

"You really changed your idea about stopping power after Laraby. After Laraby, no one should have blamed you about Dennison."

"No one really did. Except maybe McIlwain. Maybe I should have fought harder. I just didn't want to tarnish the force. I told him about Laraby, but he refused to see the connection. Laraby was some kind of zombie."

"You could hold a gun point-blank to the guy's head, and you still wouldn't kill him."

"Dennison on the other hand . . ." Matchett looked away; and Gilbert knew that Dennison would haunt Matchett for the rest of his life. "I guess I made sure with Dennison. I didn't need another night of the living dead."

"It was a race thing."

Matchett stared across the room. He nodded toward Webb. "This job, it's boring, but I never pull a gun anymore. And I'm glad about that. No pressure. Mind you, we're a little concerned about this Cheryl Latham thing. I'm glad you're working it, Barry. It's a load off."

"Are you conducting your own investigation?"

Matchett nodded. "We're doing what we can. Mostly we've tightened security."

They talked for the next half hour. And it was good talking to Matchett again. They talked about Matchett's clean break.

"I'm sorry I never called you," said Matchett. "I hope you didn't take it the wrong way."

Gilbert shook his head. "I knew you had to work things out. They didn't have the counselling back then."

"I just didn't want the associations."

"I've got no complaints."

"You had Regina . . . and your daughters." Matchett shook his head. "God, they must be grown up by now."

"Jennifer's in university next year."

"And is Regina still teaching?"

"She's at East York Collegiate now. We're living there now. In Parkview Hills."

Matchett was impressed. "That's a nice area."

"What about you?" said Gilbert. "Did you ever get married?"

He shook his head. "No," he said. "I was living with a

woman for a while up in Red Lake . . . but I . . . I knew I was going to come back down here eventually and she wanted to stay up there, so we more or less agreed . . ." He gave Gilbert a look. "You know how it is." He glanced over at Joe. "Is that your new partner?"

Gilbert nodded. "That's him," he said. "Joe Lombardo."

"Christ, they're making them younger every year. Tell him he should try smiling once in a while."

The funeral director walked by and gave them a rather flat nod. "Joe's got something on his mind right now," said Gilbert.

"Webb looks like he's getting ready to go," said Matchett. Matchett offered Gilbert his hand. "It's been nice seeing you again, Barry. Keep me informed about Cheryl Latham."

Gilbert nodded. "The same goes for you."

They shook hands.

"And maybe when spring comes I'll dig out my baseball glove," he said. "I know you guys need the help."

Gilbert's smile widened. "You're always welcome," he said.

And then Matchett retreated to the door. So good to see him again. Brought back so many good memories from patrol. Friends from patrol were friends for life. Nothing drew two men together closer than riding around in a radio car all day.

He walked over to the table and had another sandwich. The Dennison shooting. He couldn't help thinking about it now. Three weeks after the Laraby incident. Laraby, a brute of a man, high on something, PCP maybe, getting up again and again, taking a full seven rounds in the chest before Matchett finally stopped him. Laraby, shooting at Gilbert, Gilbert taking a round in the shoulder, another in the thigh, no wonder Matchett went berserk, with Gilbert lying there in a pool of blood. They were going to give Matchett an award for the Laraby thing. But then came Dylan Dennison, a delicate and light-skinned boy from Grenada, riding around in a stolen car, having some fun, never realizing that Patrol Officer Matchett, rolling up behind him with the roof lights flashing, was jittery from the Laraby thing. Dennison reached for something in the glove compartment while Matchett walked up to the driver's side. Dennison maybe thought he could fool Matchett with whatever insurance papers happened to be in the car. And Matchett, so keyed up after killing Laraby, thought the boy had a gun in the glove compartment. Matchett pulled his own weapon, squeezed three times, made sure he did it right this time, killed an unarmed fifteen-year-old Afro-Caribbean immigrant who happened to be an honor student at Scarlett Heights Secondary. The black community had been in an uproar, and rightly so. They wanted Matchett's head and they got it. They didn't care about Laraby. They didn't care about how Matchett had saved Officer Gilbert's life. They knew nothing about the night of the living dead. They only knew about their poor dead boy. They wanted blood. And the force had to give it to them.

Enough to destroy any man's life. But he knew Matchett. Matchett bounced back. Matchett never held a grudge. His old partner said a few words to Webb then left the reception room. Matchett was a man who knew how to get on with his life. Matchett had a sense of honor and purpose. Gilbert nodded to himself. And Matchett might actually help with the Latham case. He smiled at the prospect. He and Matchett working together again. Anything was possible.

Chapter Seven

An hour after the shift was over, Gilbert and Lombardo sat in the office watching, for the eighth time, the videotape of the funeral, scrutinizing each and every single guest, knowing any of them could be Cheryl's killer. The minister finished with his graveside eulogy and the walnut casket was lowered into the ground.

"Who's that?" asked Lombardo, pointing to a tall muscular-looking woman with brown hair.

"That's Jane Ireland," said Gilbert. "Webb's personal secretary."

"Why does she keep looking at Matchett like that?"

Gilbert peered more closely. "Roll the tape ahead," he said. "There's a better view coming up."

Lombardo fast-forwarded the tape.

Jane Ireland wore one of those wraparound coats, more like a cape. And Lombardo was right. She kept looking in Matchett's direction.

"Maybe for security reasons?" suggested Lombardo.

Gilbert stared at Ireland. "No," he said, "I don't think so." He straightened his back to ease his sore lumbar and put his hands on his knees. "She's got a thing for him. Look at the way she's got her mouth, all down at the corners like that." Gilbert grinned. "You of all people, Joe, should be able to see that."

"Yeah . . . well."

Gilbert contemplated Lombardo. The man was depressed, brooding about Marsh. He needed a change. He needed something to get his mind off work.

"Why don't we stop this?" said Gilbert.

"I'm going to work all night if I have to."

"Joe, you need a break. Why don't you come over to my house for supper? Regina's making her sausage casserole. We'll open a bottle of wine and we'll get a cheesecake somewhere."

Lombardo's eyes narrowed. He looked like he was going to refuse; but then he finally nodded and a smile came to his face.

"I guess I'll get to meet that exchange student after all," he said.

They sat in Gilbert's dining room. Gilbert sat at the head of the table, with fifteen-year-old Nina to his left, and eighteen-year-old Jennifer to his right. Regina sat at the other end of the table. And sitting across from each other at Regina's left and right were Lombardo and Valerie. They were talking. The two of them. On and on and on. Joe's family was from Piedmont; Valerie came from Frankfurt. When Lombardo went to Piedmont, he often drove up to Frankfurt. Valerie was a lovely amber-haired girl, tall, slim, with freckles and green eyes; she looked more Irish than German. She wore a green turtleneck and a jade bracelet. They talked nonstop as if they were the only ones at the table. And Gilbert just sat there, wondering if this was such a good idea after all. The thirteen-year age difference didn't seem to bother them in the least. Time to cool things down a bit.

"I thought we might head back downtown, Joe," he said, "after dessert, and write up that warrant for Latham's blood."

"Dad, do you have to talk about work at the dinner table?" asked Jennifer. "Especially when we have guests?"

"I thought you said I needed a little rest," said Lombardo. "I was going to take Valerie to a club I know, maybe do a little dancing."

Gilbert thought of Valerie's parents in Frankfurt, counting on him to keep their daughter safe while she was in Canada.

"That's a lovely idea," said Regina. Gilbert gave his wife a hard stare, but she ignored him. "You two go out an' have some fun."

"Dad, can I go?" asked Jennifer.

He turned to his eldest. "The kind of club Joe goes to—"

"And me too?" chimed Nina.

"You're underage," he said, unable to stop his exasperation. "You can't go to clubs yet."

He looked to Regina for help.

"Jennifer, you have school tomorrow," said Regina.

Gilbert concentrated on Valerie. "Valerie, I thought you had something at the Goethe Institute tomorrow," he said.

Valerie looked at him blankly. "No . . ." she said. "No, nothing at all."

"Then it's settled," said Lombardo.

"Now just hang on," said Gilbert. "Isn't it getting late?"

Regina tilted her head to one side, her way of telling him to ease up. "It's only eight-thirty, dear," she said. She looked at her daughters. "Girls, could you start passing up the plates?"

The girls started handing up the plates. Joe and Valerie went back to talking. Gilbert absently gave his plate to Nina.

He got up, lifted a few serving bowls and followed Regina into the kitchen, knowing he had been defeated, knowing he was stupidly treating Valerie the way he treated his own daughters. He shook his head as he pushed his way into the kitchen. Contradictions. He had seen too many female corpses. He knew Valerie would be perfectly safe with Joe. Still . . .

As he entered the kitchen, Regina looked up at him; he could hide nothing from Regina; after twenty-two years of marriage, she could read every nuance.

"You shouldn't worry so much," she said.

He contemplated her as she placed the dishes in the dishwasher. "Am I worrying?"

"If you can't trust your own partner, who can you trust?"

He put the serving bowls on the counter. "This winter is getting to me."

She slid the loaf of Italian bread back into its paper wrapper. "Maybe next year we'll visit Howard."

Gilbert nodded. "That would be nice."

"And no helping him this time. I want you on the beach."

"I wasn't helping him. I was just offering advice."

"You manage your caseload, he'll manage his."

"We're brothers."

"Then he should give you a break. Dade County has enough detectives already. They don't need you."

He nodded. He wasn't going to get into it. She was right though; every time they went to Florida, he ended up helping Howard. "Valerie likes Joe," he said.

"He's drop-dead gorgeous, Barry," she said.

She splashed a little more wine into her glass.

"You think so?" he asked.

She nodded sagely. "Oh, yes," she said.

Gilbert frowned, but it was a playful frown. "Don't you be getting any ideas."

She smiled, walked across the kitchen with a slight sway in her hips, put her arms around him, and kissed him on the chin. "I like older guys," she said.

He backed away. "Hey, I'm not that old."

"You're older than Joe."

"I came in here thinking you'd make me feel better."

"You do feel better," she said.

He shrugged and gave her a kiss on the forehead. "I guess I do," he said.

The house on Crawford Street, in the heart of the Portuguese District, was one of those bulky, three-storey duplexes built in the late 1920s, brick, with a second-floor bay window, and a third-floor dormer. Turquoise paint flaked from the red brick, a remnant from the wave of Mediterranean immigrants back in the sixties and seventies—warm Latino souls trying to fight the grey cold by painting their houses gaudy carnival colors. Many of the Portuguese and Italians had moved away in the eighties, up to Woodbridge, an opulent but remote suburb. Still lots of Portuguese, but now also Maritimers, Newfoundlanders, down-and-outers from the East Coast trying to make good in the big city, working factory lines, driving trucks, or hiring on with roofing and painting crews.

Christmas lights still dangled from the eaves. Gilbert, waiting in his car for Detective Bob Bannatyne, took a sip of his Mister Donut coffee. Gord and Diane Danby, the tenants who rented the first and second floors, were down in Florida right now; Bob Bannatyne had a key from the landlord. Yellow police tape, having come loose at one end of the balcony, now snapped fiercely in the cold wind.

Bannatyne drove up in an unmarked Chrysler Spirit. Gilbert got out of his car. Bannatyne did the same.

Bannatyne, despite the cold, wore his customary London Fog raincoat; he was heavyset man who drank beer by the six-pack—his stomach rested like a medicine ball over his belt. He was nonetheless fit, an energetic fifty-nine who had the dour visage of a bulldog and the dedication of a true soldier. He walked over the sidewalk, his feet crunching against the densely compact snow, his shoulders seesawing back and forth with each step, his customary DuMaurier hanging from the corner of his lips. He was a gruff man, but always effective.

"Are we on planet Earth?" asked Bannatyne. "Or is this Pluto?" He cuffed Gilbert gamesomely on the shoulder. "Let's get the hell inside."

They climbed the steps. Broken slabs of drywall crowded the swaybacked porch; someone was doing work inside. Bannatyne took out his key and opened the door. They went inside.

"This is where the Danbys live," said Bannatyne. "He's an instructor at George Brown, does computers, and she's a legal secretary, a young couple, no children, just starting out." Bannatyne indicated footprints in plaster dust leading to the basement stairs. "The guy's fixing the basement. Donna lived on the third floor. She got along with the Danbys. I don't know. This is from Diane's statement. We'll have to wait until the Danbys get back from Florida for more details."

"Were the Danbys here when she was murdered?" asked Gilbert.

"They left on the sixth," said Bannatyne. "Donna was murdered on the fifth. But both of them were out when it happened. When did you say her stepsister was murdered?"

They began climbing the stairs; a brief image of Cheryl's frozen corpse flashed through his mind. "The eighteenth."

Bannatyne raised his eyebrows. "Nearly two weeks later."

They rounded the banister at the top of the stairs. Gilbert peered into sparsely furnished bedrooms; one of them had been turned into an office, another into an upstairs sitting room. Though much of the furniture looked second-hand, all of it was tasteful; the art on the walls—reproductions of Flemish masters, a few Constables, and the obligatory Van Gogh—hung in neat brass frames under glass.

"What about the neighbors?" asked Gilbert. "Did they hear anything?"

"No," said Bannatyne. "The walls are thick in these old duplexes. And my perp put his gun to a pillow. That would cut down on noise."

"And it was a Heckler and Koch?"

"We found the slug lodged in one of the floorboards. He took the brass. I don't know why he didn't take the slug. It wasn't that hard to find. Maybe he just didn't have anything to dig it out with."

They began climbing the third-floor stairs. "And you're sure the perp was male?" asked Gilbert.

"It was gangland, Barry," said Bannatyne. "Point-blank in the head with a large caliber round. I've never seen a woman kill like that. Women like knives." Bannatyne shrugged. "You know how it is."

At the top of the third-floor stairs, Bannatyne removed a piece of yellow police tape from between the banister post and the wall.

Donna Varley's apartment was essentially one large room. The name Varley. He knew it had been familiar. A serve-through wall partitioned the kitchen from the rest of the unit; she shared the second-floor bathroom with the Danbys. The ceiling followed the slope of the roof. A Venetian blind covered the dormer window.

"For someone on welfare, she sure had a lot of nice things," said Bannatyne. "I bust my butt, and I still have the same department store stuff I bought ten years ago."

Gilbert took a few steps into the room and gazed at the

chair in the corner. An expensive recliner. In off-white. Now soaked dark with dried blood, reminding Gilbert of one of those psychiatric ink-blot tests. Near the top, crusted brain tissue, skull fragments, hair. Donna Varley. The mysterious stepsister from up north. Donna Varley, gunned down in cold blood; then two weeks later, her stepsister, Cheryl Latham, most probably frozen to death on purpose in the trunk of a car, then shot in the chest. And the gun, a Heckler and Koch. Making matches. Finding connections.

"We'll have ballistics compare the bullets," said Gilbert.

"I've already done the paperwork," said Bannatyne.

"I guess it's only a formality."

"Maybe," said Bannatyne.

Outside, the wind howled through the leafless branches of the maple tree. The frost was congealed in a thick crust all around the window frame. They both looked out.

"That's depressing," said Bannatyne. "I'll be leaving you assholes to freeze your nuts off next week."

Gilbert grinned. "Freeport, isn't it?"

"Actually, it's Pimento Beach, just west of Freeport."

"Which one is that on?" asked Gilbert. "I get them all mixed up."

"Grand Bahama Island."

Bannatyne walked over to the chair; back to business.

"The toxicology came back positive for alcohol and cocaine," he said. Bannatyne looked at him quizzically. "Did you get the toxicology back on Cheryl yet?"

Gilbert shook his head. "It takes an age."

The frown came back to Bannatyne's face. "And can you believe they're going to cut staff over there," he said. "Blackstein shit his pants when he found out."

Gilbert nodded toward the chair. "So she was piss-drunk and stoned."

"Fuck, I hate that smell," said Bannatyne. "Do you smell that? Guess she lost control of her bladder when he nailed her."

"It's not so bad from over here."

"I vouchered a few grams of coke. And she had some pot in the freezer."

"A real party girl."

"Seems that way."

"So no forced entry?" said Gilbert.

Bannatyne stubbed his cigarette out on the sole of his shoe and slid the butt into his pocket; he didn't want to contaminate the crime scene.

"She knew him. She let him up. And then he blew her away. And that's where we got similarities. No forced entry at Cheryl's, right? She knew him. So they both know the perp. All we have to ask ourselves is who do they know in common."

Gilbert thought for a moment. "Latham," he said.

Bannatyne left the chair and came over to the banister. "Maybe." Bannatyne pulled out his DuMauriers, tapped one out, and stuck it in the corner of his mouth. Chain-smoking as usual. "But I was thinking maybe we have to dig deeper, go back a little further."

"Like who?"

Bannatyne shrugged. "I was thinking maybe the stepbrothers," he said. "Larry and Dean Varley. I did some checking. The older one has a record."

Gilbert rode the subway home that night; Regina needed the car to take her aging mother to a widow's meeting.

From the subway, he got the Coxwell bus. The Coxwell bus took him past the Toronto East General Hospital onto O'Connor and over the Taylor Creek Bridge. This was East York, the sleepy borough where nothing ever happened, where Gilbert owned a home in Parkview Hills above the ravine.

As he entered his quiet neighborhood, he was preoccupied, running over the Donna Varley crime scene in his head again and again. Larry and Dean Varley. He would get Lombardo to run a thorough background check. If it looked promising, he would drive up to Sudbury and visit the Varley brothers in person. He was turning right onto Prestine Heights Boulevard, the street where he lived, wondering whether it would be worth his while to go over the Varley crime scene inch by inch in the hope of discovering something Bannatyne might have missed, when he heard the roar of a car engine, saw headlights flick on up ahead, and watched a car squeal out from the curb toward him. Another teenage speed devil. But then he saw that the car was coming straight for him. He took a few quick steps toward the other side of the road, thinking the driver hadn't seen him, but the car swerved right toward him; and he knew the driver was trying to hit him.

He ran toward the curb onto the wide median beside the sidewalk, but the car jumped the curb, bashing through a snowbank, targeting him. He didn't think. Instinct took over. He jumped. Even so the car's fender tagged his thigh, sending shockwaves of pain up and down his leg as he rolled onto the front lawn of the nearest house. Someone was trying to kill him. He looked at the car as it sped away, trying to get a make on the license plate; but the number had been covered with grease or mud. Then he heard gunfire. And looking the other way, he saw Joe Lombardo, one knee to the road, taking careful aim at the escaping car's tires, saw Lombardo's Fiat parked along the curb further up, saw Valerie Breitkaupt stand up out of the passenger side of the Fiat, most of the buttons of her blouse undone. Lombardo fired again, the muzzle flash bright in the deepening dusk. The car fishtailed around the corner and disappeared toward O'Connor Drive.

Lombardo shoved his gun into his holster and ran over to Gilbert. Gilbert struggled to his feet, wincing at the pain in his thigh; at least it wasn't broken.

"Are you all right?" asked Lombardo.

Gilbert glanced at Valerie who was now hastily doing up the buttons of her blouse.

"What the hell are you doing here?" asked Gilbert.

"Can you move it okay?" asked Lombardo.

"Joe, she's only nineteen."

"I gave her a lift home from the Goethe Institute."

"I'm going to tell her mother."

Lombardo stepped back. "I can't believe this," he said. "I just saved your life, and now you're going to tell her mother."

"You're going to break her heart. Can't you be a little more careful."

Gilbert winced in sudden pain.

"Let me have a look," said Lombardo.

Lombardo knelt, pulled away Gilbert's coat, and looked at the leg. "At least it's not bleeding. You got a paint smear there. I can just see it."

Gilbert looked down the now-empty Prestine Heights Boulevard. "That was no accident," he said. "Did you see what kind of car it was? It looked like maybe the kind we're after."

Lombardo stood up and nodded. "It's a Crown Victoria," he said. "It's in our target group, third on Laird's list." He looked at Gilbert's leg. "I'll have to voucher your pants, Barry? Do you mind taking them off? They're vital evidence now."

Gilbert looked at Valerie. "What, right here?"

Lombardo grinned. "Right here."

"Yeah, yeah, very funny." Gilbert began limping toward the house. Gilbert gave him a pointed look. "What about the car?"

"I couldn't get the color," said Lombardo. "It was too dark.

It could have been blue, black, purple, grey, maybe even dark green, who knows?"

"Did you get the plate number?"

Lombardo shook his head as Valerie gave them a guilty wave from the Fiat. "Nope, sorry, I couldn't make that out either."

Chapter Eight

Gilbert drove to the Ashbridges Bay Co-operative and Workshop for the Mentally Handicapped that same evening. His leg throbbed and there was a big bruise on his thigh, but he wasn't seriously injured; in fact, this vehicular assault provided yet more evidence, especially because the Auto Squad would be able to match paint samples from his pants; and if the car was actually recovered, they could get a print of the weave of his pants from it using laser retrieval equipment. Not only that, they knew for sure the car was a Crown Victoria; also, the tire tracks left in the snow, confirmed by Laird, were Michelin XGTs. A good possibility the man driving that car tonight was the same man who had killed Cheryl.

Gilbert bumped over the streetcar tracks on Queen Street, glanced at the huge rubble pile that was once the Greenwood Race Track, and turned left on the next side street, into that area of Toronto simply know as the Beaches. The evidence was tantalizing, and as far as the Cheryl Latham case was concerned, they were now looking for a Crown Victoria.

At the Ashbridges Bay Co-op he found Judith Wendeborn, the evening supervisor, playing a game of Ping-Pong with three mentally retarded adults. He stared at Judith Wendeborn through the small window of the games room door; she was having fun and so were the handicapped adults, their faces beaming in that innocently gleeful Down's syndrome way. He hated to ruin it. But an order was an order. He snapped open his accordion-style briefcase and pulled out the murder warrant. He pushed open the door. He took a few tentative steps into the room. Judith Wendeborn looked up. He gave her a sheepish wave. She was somewhere in her thirties, but prematurely grey, with a young and pretty face but nearly white hair, tied back in a ponytail with a piece of turquoise wool. She said a few words to the other players and came over.

She smiled, but it was an uncertain smile. "I didn't expect to see you for another few weeks," she said. "Did you talk to that woman?" Judith was referring to Susan Allen.

He glanced over her shoulder. "How's Wesley doing?"

Her eyes narrowed; she could tell something was wrong. "He's settled in nicely. He's a big hit with everybody."

Gilbert looked around the room. "I don't see him," he said. "Where is he?"

She glanced at the murder warrant, unsure what it was. "He's in his room," she said. "He's building a model airplane."

"I'm afraid I'm going to have to arrest him." Gilbert presented her with the first-degree murder warrant. "My Staff Inspector gave me direct orders. I have no choice."

She scanned the document, a frown slowly coming to her face. "This is for first-degree murder," she said. "Didn't we talk manslaughter?"

"I know, but I have no choice. It's all politics. Don't worry, I'm still going after Susan Allen. We've got pressure at work." He took the document back. "You know how it is. I'm still going to work the manslaughter angle. But I'm in a bit of a jam right now. She's not cooperating. We've hardly got any evidence. I'm not sure I can get the Park to issue a warrant. I'd like to get her typewriter so we can compare . . ."

He trailed off; Judith's hands were on her hips; she looked as if she had been betrayed.

"So he really has to go?" she said.

He took a deep breath. "There's nothing I can do about it."

She stared at him a moment more then glanced away. "The sad thing is, he doesn't remember any of it. Or maybe that's a good thing."

They left the games room and walked down the hall to the ward.

"Try and be nice about it," said Judith Wendeborn. "He talks about his mother all the time. He keeps asking when he's going home to see her."

Gilbert nodded. "Don't worry," he said. He pulled a Mars Bar from his pocket. "I've got a bribe."

She gave him a glum smile.

At room 106, Judith opened the door. The room smelled of LePage's plastic cement. Wesley Rowe, five-feet-six, 180 pounds, sat at the desk in an old cotton shirt and a pair of Wrangler jeans he wore too low at the hip. He turned around. His hair was brushed back from his forehead. His face was small, with his features seeming to be pushed near the middle, and his chin was so tiny and ill-defined it was all of a piece with his neck. He smiled, revealing brown and crooked teeth. He looked forty years old, but there was nothing savvy or experienced about his eyes. He didn't suffer from Down's syndrome, but he was definitely simple.

"Hi, Wesley," said Judith. "Look who came to see you."

Wesley waved. "Hi, sir," he said.

"Hello, Wesley." Gilbert glanced at the model. "What do you have there?" he asked. "A Spitfire?"

"I don't know," said Wesley. "It's an airplane."

"My father flew one of those during the war," said Gilbert.

Wesley looked at the airplane doubtfully. "Wouldn't he be too big to fit inside?" he said.

Gilbert and Judith looked at each other. Gilbert took a step closer and put his hand on Wesley's shoulder.

"Remember how I told you I was going to take you to police headquarters some day?" he said. "You said you really wanted to see it."

Wesley's eyes widened expectantly. "You mean we're going?" he said.

Gilbert glanced at Judith; he hated this duplicity.

"If it's okay with Judith," he said.

Wesley turned to Judith. "Can I go, ma'am?"

Judith lost her smile. She turned to Gilbert. "Look after him," she said. "Don't let anything bad happen to him."

Gilbert lost his own smile. What she asked was impossible.

Lombardo came to his desk and put a mimeographed copy of a Ministry of Transport record on his desk.

"Look at this," he said. "Those are the registration papers for a 1994 midnight blue Crown Victoria. Look at the name."

Gilbert glanced over the document.

Then he looked up at his partner. "Daniel Shirmaly?" he said. "Who the hell is Daniel Shirmaly?"

Lombardo's eyes narrowed. "That's Danny," he said. "Latham's Danny. His gardener, his chauffeur, whatever you want to call him. He owns a Crown Victoria."

Gilbert looked at the papers again. "So we ask him where

he was the night of the eighteenth, and if he has no alibi, we investigate."

Lombardo nodded. "I looked into car rental companies, too," he said. "Budget and Tilden rent the Crown Victoria in Ontario. I had them check their records. Guess what? Larry Varley's got one out. He's had it out since the seventh."

"Really?"

"Yeah."

"And returned it when?"

"He hasn't," said Lombardo.

Gilbert stared up at the dozens of court briefs in red binders on the shelf.

"I might take a drive up to Sudbury," he said. "To check out the Varleys. Maybe you can check Danny out while I'm gone."

"Sure."

"And see if you can dig a little more on Susan Allen." Gilbert felt the cold winds of his cynicism returning. He looked up at Lombardo, trying to hide the big sadness he felt about the Wesley Rowe case, but he couldn't manage it. The two detectives stared at each other. They were more than just partners; they were friends. "I feel bad about Wesley," he said.

Lombardo nodded, commiserating. "I know you do, Barry," said Lombardo. "I'll do what I can." Lombardo glanced out the window where the sky was clear and crisp. He scratched his head, his eyes again narrowing, a faint grin coming to his face. Lombardo, ever at ease, a man of grace and charm, now seemed awkward about something. "I did some checking into Heckler and Koch ownership province-wide," he said. Lombardo hesitated, reluctant. "You're not going to believe this, but Alvin Matchett owns a Heckler and Koch."

Gilbert stared at his partner, all expression leaving his face. "So?" he said.

Lombardo stared back; Gilbert could nearly hear the air crackle with crossed signals. "I know, Barry, but . . ." He glanced apprehensively toward the front of the office, where Carol Reid walked by with a few packages of Xerox paper. Then he turned around, put his hands on the edge of Gilbert's desk, leaned forward, and lowered his voice. "We have to at least look at it. I know he was your partner, and I know you're great friends, but—"

"Come on, Joe, you're not actually suggesting Alvin had anything to do with Cheryl's murder."

"No," said Joe, the single syllable dropping from his mouth like a brick. "Not at all. I know Alvin. I know he's a good cop. But we got to put it in the paperwork. He's a registered Heckler and Koch owner. And he has a connection to Cheryl. We ask to take a look at his gun, we have ballistics fire it a few times, and we'll file the report under J." Lombardo stood up. "When Marsh looks at the file, he'll know we've tried everything. If Alvin's the way you say he is, he'll give you his gun without a blink."

At eleven o'clock that same morning, Gilbert, accompanied by a blood technician, and with an escort of two uniforms, pulled up in front of Charles Latham's opulent home in Rosedale. Against the brilliant blue but bitterly cold sky, surrounded by snow-covered spruces and pines, Latham's house, despite its architectural dissonances, looked picturesque. Gilbert got out of his Lumina and walked back to the patrol car. The uniformed driver rolled down his window. Sometimes he longed for patrol. Arrests and collars were always so straightforward on patrol. There was never any labyrinth, maze, or dead-end.

"Keeping warm?" asked Gilbert.

The officer nodded. "You want us out for this one?" he asked.

Gilbert shook his head. "I don't think so. Maybe just park in the driveway so he knows you're here." Gilbert looked at the box of Country Style donuts sitting between the two officers. "And save one of those for me."

The driver smiled. "Will do."

The officer rolled up his window and drove into the driveway.

Gilbert walked back to his own car. The evidence technician, Monica Chavez, got out of the car with the blood-taking kit.

"You ready?" he asked.

She nodded. "Sure."

They walked up the front walk. Gilbert rang the doorbell. A moment later, Sally answered.

She looked first at Gilbert, then at Monica. Her shoulders tensed, not much, but enough for someone like Gilbert to look twice.

"Detective Gilbert," she said, now forcing a smile. "Is Mr. Latham expecting you?"

From inside the house he heard the sound of the dishwasher humming. "No," said Gilbert, pinning an apologetic grin to his face. "No, but if you wouldn't mind getting him."

She peered past his shoulder where she saw the patrol car and the two uniforms sitting in the driveway. The smile disappeared from her face.

"He's very busy," she said. "And I don't think it's a good idea to bother him about Cheryl right now."

"This shouldn't take long," he said. "If you'll just have him come downstairs we'll get it over with as quickly as possible."

Sally looked at Monica then back to Gilbert. She opened the door further, her face both anxious and puzzled. Yet the small knit in her brow indicated she was annoyed as well. "Come in," she said. "If you could just wait in the hall." No coffee or Chelsea bun this time. She was glum. Her sunny Filipino features had hardened. "I'll see if he's available."

Gilbert took a deep breath. "Sally, things will go quicker if you tell him he hasn't got a choice."

This stopped her. She gave him one last look, not a particularly hostile one, but as if she finally understood he meant business. She nodded then disappeared up the stairs.

He and Monica sat on the upholstered bench.

"Nice place," said Monica.

"He's an architect."

"I didn't know architects made so much money."

Gilbert thought of his own salary. "I guess some do."

Latham made no fuss when he came downstairs. He glanced briefly over the warrant, then simply unbuttoned his sleeve and rolled it up.

"I'm sorry about this, Charles," said Gilbert, as Monica tied the rubber tourniquet around Latham's bicep and had him make a fist.

Latham looked even paler than usual. "Was there much blood?" he asked.

Gilbert stared at Latham. Was this an act? Come on, Charles. Show me something. Let me see you. What exactly were you searching for when you tossed your wife's apartment on the night of the eighteenth? Did you borrow Danny's car?

"Enough to give us a scientifically reliable sample," said Gilbert.

Monica slid the needle into Latham's arm.

Later that afternoon, Gilbert drove to the Canadian National Institute for the Blind. Nestled among the heavily wooded parklands and ravines surrounding the old McLean Estate, just north of the Sunnybrook Health Sciences Centre, the CNIB was a sprawling network of ivy-covered buildings, dormitories, and wings. It was here that books were turned into braille, Seeing Eye dogs taught to guide, and the blind habituated to a life among the sighted.

Gilbert parked his car and hurried through the gate to the main building. Much of the CNIB was staffed by the blind, and it was odd for Gilbert to see so many of them in one place, stepping briskly along the halls, keeping to the right, their white canes gingerly held out before them, navigating their way through the corridors, up and down stairs, in and out of offices and meeting rooms as if they were completely sighted. He felt strange, like he was invisible; no one could see him; if one of them got too close he simply stepped out of the way. He finally found his way to the cafeteria.

Shirley Chan waited for him at a table by the window eating Chinese noodles out of a Tupperware container, not with chopsticks but with a fork, and sipping a Diet Coke. He worked his way around the tables, careful not to step on the tails of the many guide-dogs. They had never met, but he knew who she was from the funeral surveillance, and from Sonia Bailey's description. He stopped in front of her table and leaned forward.

"Ms. Chan?" he said.

She was thirty-five, with black bangs cut straight across her eyebrows, an attractive woman, wearing red lipstick, a jade necklace, and a silk blouse with small yellow dragons.

"Detective Gilbert," she said.

He pulled out his shield and nodded. "Thanks for getting back to me so quickly," he said.

"Anything I can do to help," she said. She wasn't native Chinese, had to be at least second-or-third generation, spoke with a plain Canadian accent. "We're all still stunned around here," she said. "Cheryl was liked by everybody."

Gilbert opened his briefcase and took out his notebook. "I'm sorry about Cheryl, Ms. Chan."

"Call me Shirley."

"I understand you were good friends with her."

Shirley glanced out the window where the bare branches of a maple tree scraped against the pane. "I was her friend," she said. "But she had a certain reserve. I don't know if I ever got through that reserve."

Gilbert flipped to a fresh page of his notebook. "And she was at work on the seventeenth? You saw her here on that Monday?"

Shirley nodded. "She was here."

"And did she seem different to you at all?"

Shirley took a deep breath. "I'm not sure how to answer that. Not different from the way she'd been behaving lately."

Gilbert's eyes narrowed and he leaned forward. "How do you mean?"

Shirley absently stirred her noodles with her fork.

"I don't know, maybe she was just overworked. She worked so hard. She lived for work. At one point last year she was holding two jobs."

"She was?"

"Her stepfather hired her as a fund-raising consultant. A six-month contract."

"Because of the election," said Gilbert.

"She's a bit of an expert. She knows how to raise money." Shirley ate a mouthful of noodles, chewed meditatively, stared out the window. "She must have been working sixteen-hour days. Maybe it was just because she was so tired . . . since Christmas . . . I don't know. She hasn't been as chipper. She had an affair. With someone from her stepfather's staff. It didn't turn out well. And she had family problems. Not that she would ever tell anyone about them. She was a private . . ."

Shirley Chan put her fork down and stared at Gilbert. "You know what I mean? You could spend a whole day with Cheryl and not be any wiser. She had this guard, this suit of armor she put on. To tell you the truth, I found it exasperating at times."

"You say she had an affair," said Gilbert. "With who?"

A few of the sighted employees walked by with trays of food, glancing curiously at their table. When it came to murder, everyone was curious.

"A man named Alvin Matchett," she said.

Gilbert felt his face turning red. "Alvin Matchett," he repeated.

"Yes." She took a sip of her Diet Coke through her white plastic straw. "A very nice guy. She should have worked harder. I don't know what happened. First Charles, then Alvin, she can't seem to stick it through."

"You met Alvin Matchett?" he said.

"Twice," she said. "She couldn't have chosen a sweeter guy. A real gentleman. I think she regretted the way things turned out."

"She was upset about it?"

"I think so. But she didn't talk about it. She lost some weight. And she looked awful. I told her, go see a doctor. But she doesn't like doctors. She doesn't like people poking and prodding her."

He looked out the window, where three grackles settled on the branch of the maple tree. Why didn't Matchett mention this? Then again, why should he? It was over and done with. Still, he would have to ask Alvin about it.

"And do you know Charles?" asked Gilbert.

She raised her eyebrows. "A bit," she said.

"And what do you think?"

Her face settled. "I find him moody," she said. "He loses

his temper easily. I once saw him smash a four-hundred-dollar vase because he didn't like where Cheryl put it."

Gilbert contemplated Shirley Chan. Something not right about Latham, that's for sure, and Shirley was confirming it.

"Is that it?" he asked.

She took a deep breath, now reluctant. "He was always snooping," she said. "At least that's the impression I got. Whenever he came to the office here, he would pull open filing cabinets and look through them, really inappropriate, right in front of everybody, stuff that was none of his business. We didn't know what to say. I mean, what do you say to a man like that, a man who has absolutely zero social grace?"

Gilbert's eyes narrowed. "Did he do this often?" he asked.

"Often enough." A wary crease came to her brow. "But I can't help thinking . . ." She looked down at her noodles. Then she looked up at Gilbert, her eyes now inquisitive. "You knew about the burglary, didn't you?"

As if, because he was a detective, he knew about every one of the hundreds of burglaries committed every month in Metro.

"What burglary?" he said, frowning a bit.

"Our office was burgled the night Cheryl was murdered."

He assimilated this information calmly, evaluating it as perhaps a major piece of evidence. Cheryl's murder had a contralateral crime; the murder of her stepsister, Donna Varley. Now there seemed to be a contralateral crime to the tossing of Cheryl's apartment. He would phone Richter in Burglary and get the details.

"And was anything taken?"

"No," she said, and she now looked perplexed. "Nothing at all."

Chapter Nine

Alvin Matchett wouldn't meet Gilbert at police head-quarters. Though the changeover in staff had been considerable in the last fifteen years, there were still many officers and detectives who remembered Matchett, and who couldn't forget the Dennison shooting. Likewise, Matchett didn't want Gilbert to come to the Parliament Buildings, especially with Ronald Roffey sniffing around. So they met in Queen's Park, just north of the legislature. Temperatures had climbed, the winds had died, and the sun shone benevolently as they strolled the path toward the War Memorial.

Gilbert was apologetic but insistent; Matchett was grave but cooperative.

"It ended four months ago," said Matchett. "It was stupid. I didn't know what I was thinking. The whole thing was a mistake."

"And Jane didn't like it," said Gilbert.

"She and I were . . . up until last June. But then I just got . . . I got tired of it all. The fitness thing, the vitamins, and the food, it was just too much for me. I'm getting old. Jane's forty-two, she still thinks she can fight it, but she's going to learn sooner or later."

"So you and Jane—"

"For nearly two years. I actually lived with her for a while. You should see the biceps on her. She can bench-press two-hundred-and-fifty pounds. She's got . . . and her pecs . . . anyway, we split up, and Jane took it hard, but I felt . . . I don't know, I felt great. No more fighting free radicals by mega-dosing with antioxidants."

Up ahead, an old man in a grey overcoat and fingerless gloves, his nose as red as a strawberry and as large as a tomato, fed bread crumbs to pigeons from a plastic bag. Students from the nearby Faculties of Music and Law strolled the park, enjoying the unexpected thaw.

"So when did you start seeing Cheryl?" asked Gilbert. "I don't mean to be nosy, but you know how it is."

"I've got nothing to hide."

Gilbert recognized the refrain from the Dennison hearings.

"She came on staff about the end of May," said Matchett. "I thought when Tom hired her he was doing her a favor, you know, family and everything. But she was qualified. She was a good fund-raiser, not only helped Tom's campaign but the whole Tory campaign. That's where we really got to know each other. Working the money thing for her stepfather. It was like our personal crusade."

Out on Queen's Park Crescent, a delivery truck backfired. The pigeons the old man was feeding leaped into the air and swept over Gilbert and Matchett. Matchett jerked to one side and ducked, raising both hands above his head. Gilbert stared at his old partner. Matchett looked up at the pigeons with phobic aversion.

"You've got a thing about birds?" asked Gilbert.

Matchett lowered his arms, watching the pigeons apprehensively as they circled back to the old man and the bread crumbs.

"I hate them," he said. "I always have."

"Then I'll take back the budgie I got you for your birthday."

"Good," said Matchett. "Get me a cat instead."

"I thought you were allergic to cats."

"I am," he said. "But they make great bird killers."

Gilbert laughed.

They strolled to the other side of the park in silence, both of them in their own thoughts. An old Chinese couple practiced Tai Chi under a tree in the snow. When Gilbert and Matchett reached the War Memorial, Gilbert pointed across the street.

"That's my car over there," he said. "In the Law School parking lot. You're sure you have enough time for this? I can come back after work if you want?"

Matchett watched the traffic, waiting for a break. "You just want the gun, right?"

Gilbert nodded. "That's all."

"Then we should have plenty of time."

The Avenue Road bus rumbled by. They hurried across in the wake of the bus and entered the Law School parking lot. A young man stepped gingerly through the ice-covered lot carrying a double bass, coming from the Faculty of Music directly behind the Law School. Gilbert and Matchett got in Gilbert's Lumina.

"What's the best way?" asked Gilbert.

"Back down to Wellesley and across. Then right on Parliament to Winchester."

Gilbert started the car.

As they drove eastbound on Wellesley, they resumed their discussion.

"Anyway, Jane was jealous," said Matchett. "She wouldn't

cooperate. This was her response to the whole thing, her way of getting back. Not that she was much involved with the election. She was too busy running Tom's office, handling the day-to-day stuff. But when we needed help, she was a real pain. Say we needed a car at a certain location at a certain time. Before Cheryl, she'd go to the carpool herself and deliver it personally. Not later on. Sometimes we'd be lucky to get a car at all. Or if we had a pile of stuff to fax, she'd always get it out late and she'd pin the blame on Cheryl. I don't know why. As if making my life inconvenient was going to change things. I still have clothes over at Jane's place. I've been trying to arrange a time to go over and get them. No dice. I think I'm just going to have to wait until she cools down."

They caught the red light at Church Street, in the heart of the gay section; several slim young men with short hair and mustaches strode by; Gilbert couldn't help wondering, why short hair and mustaches all the time?

"You don't think . . ." He faltered. "I mean she was jealous, but she was jealous in a normal way. She didn't flip out."

Matchett looked at him with a mocking grin. "You know, with you around, everybody in this city is going to be a suspect sooner or later. Jane may have her idiosyncrasies, but she's not whacka-whacka."

"But she came back to earth, didn't she?" said Gilbert. "Once you and Cheryl split."

Matchett took a deep breath, thinking it over. "She got a little better." He stared at the dashboard, thinking. "Then again, I still haven't got my clothes back."

"Why exactly did you and Cheryl end it?"

The light turned green and they eased across the intersection.

"I guess when the election was over there just didn't seem to be any fizz left," said Matchett. "We had nothing to talk about. We had no real mutual interests. We made no conscious decision to end it. We just more or less went back to our other lives. We picked up old patterns, and those patterns didn't include each other. Her stepsister moved from Sudbury about that time. I guess her stepsister had troubles of one kind or another. I was sorry to hear about her murder."

"Did you ever meet Donna?"

"I met the lot of them. Her stepbrothers came down in early December, I don't know why, family meeting of some kind. I can't say that Donna and Larry are my kind of people. I don't mean to be . . . you know . . . I tried to like them, but I just found them . . . I don't know, trashy. Real down-and-outers, losers with dirty hair and bad teeth. Dean was all right, though. I think he's a dentist or something."

They passed the government-subsidized high-rises of Jamestown and turned right on Parliament. A family meeting. Gilbert would have to make a note of that. He was beginning to think Bannatyne was right; maybe their prime suspects in both murders might turn out to be the Varley brothers.

They turned left on Winchester past the old Winchester Hotel, with its cheap draft, cheap drunks, and cheap rooms, a leftover from Cabbage Town, when the area was still the city's worst slum, before all the trendies and yuppies invaded.

"I'm right here," said Matchett, pointing to a huge Edwardian house. "I have the whole third floor."

Gilbert found a parking spot along the curb. "I still haven't figured out Cheryl's family tree. Dorothy was her birth mother?"

"That's right."

"So Dorothy married Craig Shaw, and together they had Cheryl. Joe's still digging through the Registrar's records. We're still trying to piece it together."

"Craig Shaw was a big shot with Lac Minerals, back when Lac Minerals was still a going concern. He was killed in a cave-in touring one of their new operations in Quebec."

"That much we've learned."

"Cheryl was around ten at the time."

"Any other children from that marriage?"

Matchett unsnapped his seat-belt. "Nope," he said, "Cheryl's the only one."

The two men got out of the Lumina and headed across the street. God, that sun felt nice.

"So Dorothy then married Paul Varley," said Gilbert.

Matchett nodded. "Some time in the early seventies."

"And he already had three children."

Matchett pushed the gate open. "Larry and Dean were quite a bit older. Larry was nineteen and Dean was seventeen. Then again, Donna was younger than Cheryl. Cheryl was twelve when her mother married Paul Varley. Donna had to be about nine."

"And were things all right?" asked Gilbert. "Did Cheryl get along with her new family?"

They went up the walk. Matchett took out his house keys.

"As far as I know, yes," he said. "I don't think she was ever that close to the boys. They were so much older. Larry was already moved out. And Dean, I don't know, I think he left for Guelph a year later. He went to school there. So it was really only Donna. Donna's not too terribly bright. I think Cheryl must have dominated her."

He opened the door and they went inside. "So then Paul Varley died," said Gilbert.

"About two years later," said Matchett. "In a snowmobile accident. Apparently the girls were with him. They were miles from nowhere, up in Onaping Falls. The girls weren't hurt, but by the time they got help, Paul Varley was already dead."

Gilbert shook his head. "That's too bad."

"Kind of rough, isn't it?" said Matchett, as they began climbing his private set of stairs to his third-floor apartment. "To lose two fathers in the space of four years. But Cheryl's resilient. The more you get to know her, the more you see that. She's got a tough little spot inside her nobody can touch."

"And her mother married Webb when?"

"Some time in the mid-eighties. Donna stayed in Sudbury. She wanted to be close to her brothers, even though by that time Larry had been in and out of jail a number of times. Tom has his constituency up there, but when he became the member for Sudbury West, they moved down here. Cheryl wanted to be with her mother. And she wanted to go to school here so it all worked out."

They climbed the second flight of stairs to Alvin Matchett's apartment. The building had been newly renovated and the hardwood steps gleamed. Matchett opened the door and they went inside. The more Gilbert thought about it, the more he realized he would have to drive up to Sudbury.

"I keep it in the bedroom," said Matchett, flicking on the light.

"Do you want me to take off my shoes?" asked Gilbert.

"No, it's all right. I'll just be a second."

Matchett hurried down the hall. Gilbert glanced around while he waited. The mishmash of furnishings in the living room, the way they looked so hastily arranged, gave the place an impermanent unlived-in look. Peering into the kitchen, Gilbert saw three pizza boxes stuffed between the fridge and the counter and a half-finished frozen dinner on the table.

Matchett returned from his bedroom carrying what looked like a metal attaché case.

"You just want the gun, right?" he said. "You don't need the case."

"Maybe a couple of your rounds to test-fire."

"Sure."

Matchett lifted the snaps and opened the case.

And they both just stared.

114

The gun wasn't there. Only its hard-foam case impression, as detailed as a foundry mold, cut cleanly in the perfect shape of a Heckler and Koch .45, but empty, gone, taken. The eleven-round clip was there, snug in its own perfect little mold. So were the custom shoulder mount, the owner's manual, the registration papers, a can of gun oil, two tins of ammunition, and the gun club schedule. But the actual weapon was gone.

Gilbert looked at Matchett, waiting for an explanation, waiting for him to go back to his bedroom and maybe find the semiautomatic in his dresser drawer. But Matchett just stared at the empty mold in disbelief. Then Matchett turned to Gilbert; it was like the two of them were rock climbing; and Gilbert was already at the top pulling Matchett up by a rope; but now the rope snapped; and Matchett's expression was frozen in that instant of the snapping rope, with the realization he was falling, and that there was nothing Gilbert could do to save him. Matchett looked at the empty case again, as if he had to convince himself. Gilbert waited patiently.

"Barry, this is . . ." Matchett's face flushed, and he turned quickly away, rubbing his hand over his brow, his mouth slackening in astonishment, the veins above his temples bulging. "Barry, the gun was there. You know me. I'm careful about firearms. The gun was there, I know it was. I do everything by the book. The only time that gun comes out of the case is at the range."

"Maybe you were cleaning it," suggested Gilbert. "Maybe you left it in your bedroom somewhere."

Matchett gave his head a brief shake, dismissing the idea outright.

"I never clean it here," he said. "We have a workbench at the club. I always . . ."

He looked down the hall, clutching at the remote possibility that he may indeed have cleaned his gun here after all. He broke suddenly away from Gilbert and hurried to his bedroom. He ducked quickly inside. Gilbert, hearing him pull open dresser drawers, followed quietly behind. He stopped at Matchett's bedroom door. Matchett ferreted madly through underwear and socks, opened the next drawer, looked through sweatpants and sweaters, opened the next drawer, searched through pants and shorts. Then went to his closet, opened the built-in drawers there. Then checked under his bed. Got desperate. Under the pillows. Finally between the mattress and the box spring. Then stopped, walked to the window, checked the ledge, kicked a pile of clothes out of the way, put his palms against the sill, and leaned forward, staring out the pane at the sunny street below, as if he believed the gun might be out on the roof.

"Alvin . . ." Gilbert didn't know what to say.

Matchett whirled around. "If you think I had anything to do with the murder of Cheryl Latham, you're crazy. Why would I murder Cheryl? There's no reason at all."

"Alvin . . . no one said anything . . . I know you didn't murder Cheryl . . . but we have to find the gun . . . do you have any idea . . ."

"Of course I don't," he said. "If I knew where it was, I'd give it to you."

"So you think someone might have taken it?" asked Gilbert. "When was the last time you were up at the gun club?"

"A week ago Thursday," he said. "I go every Thursday night."

"But you weren't there last Thursday night?"

"No," he said. "I was too busy going over the security measures for the funeral."

"So the last time you saw the gun in the case was that Thursday night up at the gun club?"

"Yes."

Gilbert thought for a moment; so the Heckler and Koch was last seen six days before the murder.

"Any sign of a break-in?" suggested Gilbert. "You don't think someone could have burgled your apartment for the gun."

"We used to work break-ins, Barry," he said. "I don't think I'd miss it."

"How many people know you own the gun?"

Matchett moved away from the window and sat on the end of the bed. "I don't know," he said, his voice now growing despondent. "Everyone at the club. Everyone at work. Otto."

Gilbert raised his eyebrows. "Otto Kovacs?"

Matchett nodded.

"I didn't know he was still around."

"He was out West for a while but he's moved back."

"I don't know how long it's been. Twenty-five years at least. I should look him up."

"Still the same old Otto. He works for Hydro now."

"So Otto knows you have the gun. Who else?"

Matchett shook his head absently, his eyes widening in bewilderment. "That's it. That's everybody. I don't know who's taken it, but obviously someone's taken it."

"Someone with a key? Who else has a key to this place?"

Matchett's eyes narrowed; he hesitated. "Just my landlord," he said.

"Are you sure?"

"Of course I'm sure."

"Because if you're not sure, I think you better let me know."

"It doesn't have to be someone with a key," he said irritably. "I don't live a hermit's life here, Barry. I have people in and out all the time. I don't think anyone I know would steal my gun, but you never know."

"We've really got to find that gun, Alvin."

"I'll report it stolen. I've got the serial number."

"And I'm going to have to know where you were on the night of Cheryl's murder."

Matchett sprang up. "This is starting to sound like Dennison, you know that? You're turning me into a suspect. Do you have any idea what I went through with Dennison? Do you have any idea what it's like to have your whole career ruined just because of one little mistake? And now it's happening all over again. Circumstances are ganging up on me. I finally found a job I like and that I can live with, and the hallowed MTPF is going to rip it all apart again. I should have been reinstated after the Dennison enquiry. I shot him, I admit it, I shot him even though he was unarmed, but for Christ's sake, Barry, he looked like he was reaching for something. And the car came up as stolen. How was I to know he was just a fifteen-year-old black kid going for a joy ride? There's not one day that goes by I don't think about that kid. Not one single day."

"I know, Alvin," said Gilbert. "But we still have to find the gun."

"Shoot any one of those bastards on the enquiry in the chest the way Laraby did to me, and you would have seen a much different ruling," said Matchett. "I would have been like you by now. I would have been in Homicide."

"I know, Alvin," said Gilbert. "You're a damn good cop."

"I was one of the best."

"So you have to understand that I have to follow this procedure."

"I didn't kill Cheryl."

"No one says you did."

"Give me the case file, Barry. I'll find her killer."

"You know I can't do that, Alvin."

"Give me the file, I'll drag the prick in. I'm not going to go through another Dennison."

Gilbert clasped his old partner's shoulder and gave it a gentle shake. "We're just going to straighten things out, that's all."

Matchett stared at the floor, not saying a word. He was breathing fast, huffing, and his face was blotchy; Gilbert knew just how deeply scarred his old partner had been by the whole Dennison affair. He glanced out the window, where he saw a diaper truck drive by. Matchett's breathing grew a little easier.

"All right?" said Gilbert.

Matchett continued to stare at the floor but finally nodded. Gilbert took his hand off his shoulder.

"Good," he said. "Now just tell me where you were on Tuesday night."

Matchett shrugged but it was a hopeless shrug. "I got off work late. We were expecting a protest over the announced cuts but I guess because it was so cold that day it never materialized. I didn't go straight home. I went to Lanyon's for supper. That's just down here on Parliament, south of Gerrard. Talk to Cindy, she was my waitress. Then I came home for a while and watched TV."

"Did anybody hear or see you come in?"

"I don't know. I have a private entrance."

Gilbert considered. "So you got home from Lanyon's about eight."

"About that."

"And you watched TV."

"Until about ten. Then I went to the Winchester and had a few drinks."

"So no one can confirm where you were between nine and ten."

Matchett shrugged, as if it were a matter of no great concern to him. "I thought you said Cheryl got back from fitness class just after nine. What difference does it make whether someone knows where I was between nine and ten?"

"And people can confirm you were at the Winchester at ten."

"All of the regulars know me. You can ask any of them."

"And what time did you leave the Winchester?"

"About eleven," said Matchett.

"And you went straight home?"

Matchett nodded, now growing impatient. "I went straight home. And I'm sorry, no one saw me come in. Maybe someone downstairs heard me. You can check with them. They're nice people. Quiet types. Early risers. They might have been in bed by that time."

"You didn't phone anybody?"

"No."

Gilbert scratched his forehead. "Okay, okay," he finally said. "I don't think there's anything to worry about. You give me a list of everybody who knows you have that gun." He glanced at his watch. "Shit, look at the time. I better get you back to work."

"You're going to look for the gun?" asked Matchett.

"What choice do I have?"

"Barry, I didn't do it."

"I know you didn't. But I've got to have the paperwork, Alvin."

"So I'll give you this list and you'll go around accusing all my friends of theft?"

"Don't worry. I'll be diplomatic."

When they were in the car driving back, they again caught the light at Church and Wellesley. A cross-dresser walked by, beautiful, attractive, slim, with ruby red lipstick and false eyelashes, but with the obvious big hands of a man.

"And you're sure no one else has a key to your apartment?" said Gilbert.

Matchett's face settled. "No," he said. "No one at all."

*   *   *

At three o'clock that afternoon, Joe Lombardo dropped the evening edition of the *Toronto Star* on his desk.

"That asshole Roffey is at it again," he said.

The story occupied five inches of column on the third page, no longer first-page material the way it had been last week. Gilbert read the lead:

POLICE SAY NO SUSPECTS IN CHERYL LATHAM SLAYING

He read no further.

"Where did he get that?" he asked. "Did he not read our statement?"

"I guess he wants names."

"Fuck him," said Gilbert. "He's not getting names. He's trying to force our hand. Like he always does."

"Carol says Ling was by," said Lombardo. "I wasn't here at the time. But he talked to Marsh for at least thirty minutes. And now Marsh wants to see us."

"Right now?"

Lombardo nodded. "That's why I'm here. Carol's already brought him the file."

Gilbert glanced at his computer, where dozens of little Windows logos floated out from the screen. "Shit," he said. "I told her if she wants a file she has to ask me first. I'm going to start keeping things on disk. To hell with this hardcopy shit."

"She had no choice," said Lombardo. "Marsh wanted it. She had to get it. I'm afraid you're number-two tyrant around here, Barry."

Gilbert made a face. "Very funny."

"Not if you're Carol."

Marsh flipped impatiently through the case file, examining photographs, double-checking measurements, reading only the external-marks-of-violence and cause-of-death sections in the autopsy report. He had his own copy of the *Toronto Star* at his elbow, folded neatly to page three. A cigarette smoldered in an ashtray next to a smoke-eater—officially there was no smoking in the new building. He had the Donna Varley file on his desk as well, open to the ballistics section. But what seemed to interest him the most was the Cheryl Latham crime-scene report. He took one last look at the crime-scene report then shoved everything aside.

"You've read this shit Roffey wrote?" he said.

Both detectives nodded. "We have suspects, Bill," said Gilbert. "We just don't want to name them yet. We don't have enough information to conduct a useful interrogation yet."

"You guys should have been at the interrogation stage a week ago," said Marsh.

Both detectives looked at each other. Lombardo said, "Bill, this is a little more complicated than a domestic." He gestured toward the crime-scene report. "The complexity of the crime scene should tell you that."

"What's so complex about it? You've got an outdoor crime scene, everyone knows that's hell on wheels, but so what? Deal with it."

"I don't think that's what Joe means, Bill."

Marsh gave Gilbert a withering look. "Well maybe you better tell me what he means, Barry. I guess I'm just stupid or something. I guess I didn't have two years of architectural school. Why don't you spell it out for me?"

"Come on, Bill," said Gilbert. "Don't be like that."

"I get Ling, comes in here ready to shove bamboo shoots up my fingernails, and you tell me don't be like that? I'm facing eighteen percent in cuts, my clearance rate has hit rockbottom, and maybe Ling's starting to think I'm the problem, that I'm the one who has to go. And now you're telling me this is a complex crime scene. So why don't you explain it to me, Einstein. I guess I went to stupid school. I just don't get it." Marsh stood up and walked to the window. His face was red and his shoulders were hunched as he gazed across the street at the trendy College Park shopping complex. He had a brittle and overwhelmed look to his hard blue eyes. "Look . . . guys. . . ." He turned around, seeming to deflate. "I'm sorry." He glanced at Lombardo, but didn't really see him, as if to Marsh, Lombardo really wasn't in the room. "I realize the scene is a little strange. I'm sorry I blew up like that. But Ling can be such a prick." He tapped the crime-scene report. "I think what you have to answer here," he said, now looking at Gilbert, "is why your perp moved the body from Cherry Beach to Dominion Malting. If she was already dead, why bother to move her? Why not just leave her on the beach?"

Gilbert and Lombardo glanced at each other. "Bill, I don't know whether that's so important," said Gilbert. "He could have moved her for any number of reasons. Maybe a car came along. A car came along and because he was still in the vicinity he thought he better hide the body. And the best place to hide the body was the trunk. He drove away from Cherry Beach and when the coast was clear he dumped her at the first available spot, which happened to be the pier at Dominion Malting. Did you get my memo about Sudbury, by the way? I E-mailed it after lunch."

"E-mailed it?" said Marsh, as if he had never heard of E-mail, and looking proud of the fact. "You expect me to read anything that comes to me by E-mail? I hardly know my password. You want me to read something, bring it to me direct."

Gilbert told Marsh about Larry and Dean Varley and why he thought it would be a good idea to go to Sudbury.

"You can't do this by phone?" asked Marsh.

"You never know what leads I might uncover up there," said Gilbert. "Leads I'll have to follow. And I can tell a lot better if someone's lying face to face than I can over the phone. I've already phoned ahead to the SRPD. They don't mind. They'll even give me backup if I need it."

"What about Latham?" said Marsh, still unsure about Gilbert's plans. "I thought you were closing in. What about this Danny guy who works for him?"

Gilbert looked at Lombardo. "Joe's working that side of the case."

Marsh peered at Lombardo skeptically. "Mr. Librarian's actually been hitting the street?"

Lombardo tried to keep a straight face but a frown got through just the same. "Two things," he said. "Danny's Crown Victoria was supposedly in the garage on the night of the murder getting a tune-up. I asked myself, who gets a tune-up in the middle of winter? Second thing, I got the test back on the paint from Barry's pants. Midnight blue, exclusive to Crown Victoria. Danny's car is midnight blue. I say to myself, this is too much. So I go to the garage and I talk to the mechanic, another Filipino guy, and he says, sure, Danny's car was in on the eighteenth. I ask to see the receipts, he says he hasn't got them. I ask, where are they? He says he doesn't know. So I ask to talk to the owner. The owner's not there right now. So I do some checking, and this garage is owned by a numbered corporation. And who should own this numbered corporation but Charles Latham. Turns out he has several small concerns around town, all under this umbrella corporation: a restaurant in Chinatown, an art gallery up in Hazelton Lanes, a barber-supply place in Mississauga. He's got his hands in everywhere." Lombardo shrugged. "So what does this say to me? Okay, maybe Danny's car was in the garage the night of the murder. I'll ask some of the other guys who work in the garage. But maybe Latham has access to this garage. Maybe he needs a car, one we can't trace; so he goes to this garage the night of the murder, and takes Danny's car.

There's a low-rise across the street. I've canvassed some of the neighbors, asking if they saw late-night activity at the garage, but so far no witnesses."

Marsh was grinning now, and his grin wasn't at all skeptical. He raised his index finger and shook it absently at Lombardo. "I like that," he said. "That's good, Joe."

Lombardo didn't exactly beam, but he was certainly happy about Marsh's reaction.

"This Crown Victoria," continued Marsh. "What color was the one Larry Varley rented?"

"Midnight blue as well," said Lombardo. "Kind of a standard color for that car."

Marsh nodded, as if he were just confirming things for himself. "This looks good. You've got to find that car. You find that car, and we solve this murder."

Lombardo pulled a three-and-a-half-inch computer disk from his shirt pocket. "The Ministry of Transportation E-mailed me every owner of every Crown Victoria in Ontario."

Marsh's grin faded. "Don't go waving those things at me."

"I've got a sorting program," said Lombardo. "I'll start with male owners who live in Toronto, and move outward."

Chapter Ten

Highway 400, extending straight north from Toronto, is more to most Torontonians than just a super highway; it's a spiritual escape route, a gateway to the north, the fabled yellow brick road to the even more fabled Cottage Country. Sweet in summer, bleak in winter. Rolling farmland south, rock and bush north. 400 forks into 69 and 11 south of Orillia, each again spiritual thoroughfares in the consciousness of Southern Ontarians, highways that lead deep into the Canadian Shield, and, in fact, enter the land of the silver birch, home of the beaver, the blue lake, the rocky shore, such as the legendary camp song canonizes. Weekend escapees strip off the urban armor of the densely populated Golden Horseshoe, that megalopolis cusping the west end of Lake Ontario; they return to the ghosts of the Iroquois and Algonquin. The fish are always biting, the wild blueberries are always ripe, and the loon call echoes across the lake at night.

As Gilbert forked left onto highway 69 and saw the first

massive slabs of granite thrusting from the stunted birch and cedar bush, his shoulders eased and his grip on the wheel loosened. The demarcation between north and south came abruptly, from farmland to rock within a few miles, a change that made Gilbert always feel as if he had left Toronto far behind. Always the same whenever he came up here; the tension melted away. The sky was overcast with thin grey clouds. The landscape was white, snow-covered, with the road blasted through rock, the iron-rich cutaways bleeding rust, blemishing the snow. Here and there, local teenagers used the sheer cuts for spray-paint graffiti, an insult to Precambrian igneous rock nearly four billion years old.

He chewed up the kilometers, thinking about the case, trying to make sense of the evidence thus far. Driving knocked the pieces of the puzzle closer. Some people got their best ideas just as they were falling asleep at night; Gilbert got his when he was driving. Latham, Danny, Sally, Larry, Dean, Alvin. Maybe Jane Ireland. If nothing else, Jane Ireland had motive. He shook his head as he neared Parry Sound. He crossed the French River, that capricious waterway Champlain had used to penetrate to the heart of Huronia. Could he draw the line there, at Jane Ireland, or did he have to go further? Tom Webb? Sonia Bailey? Even Shirley Chan? Sometimes he had to agree with Alvin. Given enough time, he would make everybody a suspect.

He let the case drift, lulled by the rhythm of the road, passing trucks when the road periodically widened into three lanes.

Soon, far in the distance, he saw a giant smokestack, the Inco superstack, the single most identifiable landmark in Sudbury, over five hundred feet high, pouring tons and tons of acid-rich steam into the sky, blighting the countryside for miles around. The Precambrian rock in and around Sudbury looked scorched, blackened by over a half century of ore processing, as bleak a landscape as could be found anywhere, with most of the trees dead or dying, the snow looking more grey than white, and the faint smell of rotten eggs hanging in the air.

Highway 69 widened to a four-lane divided highway. He passed a McDonald's, Pizza Hut, Burger King, Home Depot, and a Wal-Mart. The true north strong and free. Highway 69 hooked onto Regent Street, and finally onto Paris Street, one of the city's main drags. He turned right and headed east toward the city center.

The Sudbury Regional Police Department gave him Officer Guy Faucher as support. Faucher had a heavy French Canadian accent.

"You see there the home and work addresses of Dr. Dean Varley," said Faucher, tapping the contact sheet Gilbert held in his hands. "Also his telephone numbers. As for Mr. Larry Varley, well, detective, you can take your guess along with the rest us. He was residing at the President Hotel, in a room on the third floor—this must be the last week of January. But now he goes away. And we don't know where he goes. Maybe his brother does. Maybe his brother is a man who will help you."

As it turned out, Dr. Dean Varley wasn't a dentist, such as Matchett had suggested. He was a veterinarian.

Gilbert phoned beforehand and let Varley know he was coming.

He found the Lansing Animal Clinic at the far end of town, right near the Taxation Building in a new strip mall sandwiched between a 7-Eleven and a Wendy's. He parked, grabbed his accordion-style briefcase from the passenger seat, and got out of the car. Out on the street a flatbed truck loaded with fresh-cut timber rumbled by. Small snowflakes, really just pellets, fell from the slategrey sky. This was Tom Webb's riding, Sudbury West, solidly working class, most of the men miners, loggers, or pulp and paper workers. He approached the clinic, passing a group of French-speaking high-school students. So many French-Canadians in Sudbury. A lot of native Ojibwa as well. He opened the door and went into the animal clinic.

The waiting area was clean, new. On the walls hung several reproductions of Robert Bateman's super-realist paintings of Canadian wildlife. Animal owners sat in chairs with either cats in cages or dogs on leashes. The receptionist, a young woman with startlingly blonde hair, wearing some kind of nurse's uniform, looked up at him with curious eyes—he was the only one in the waiting area who didn't have an animal.

"Can I help you?" she asked.

He pulled out his wallet and showed her his shield.

"I'm Detective Barry Gilbert from Toronto," he said. "I called about a half hour ago."

She nodded quickly. A solemn look came to her eyes. From somewhere in the back, Gilbert heard a dog yelp.

"Wait right here," she said.

She got up and went to the back.

Less than a minute later the door opened and out came Dr. Dean Varley. He wore a light blue doctor's tunic and smelled of strong disinfectant soap. He was short, no more than five-feet-four, but well-built, muscular, with tightly coiled brown hair, thick brown eyebrows, and intelligent eyes. He had to be forty-two, with a wide friendly face, and a chin that looked too closely shaved.

"Detective Giller?" he said.

"The name's Gilbert," said Gilbert. "Barry Gilbert."

They shook hands. "Come into the back," he said. "I've got coffee if you like."

"Thanks, I'm fine."

"Linda, hold calls for the next little while. Charlene's going to handle the routines."

"Yes, Dr. Varley."

"And if Mr. Claveau phones about his horse again, tell him the earliest I can make it is next Tuesday. Give him Dr. Hasselback's number. Dick might be able to go."

"Yes, Dr. Varley."

Gilbert followed Varley into the back. Kennels of every shape and size lined the walls. Seven or eight cats wandered freely. Gilbert glimpsed briefly a small boa constrictor coiled in a large aquarium. Two West African cockatoos squawked at each other near the back. Dr. Varley led him into an examining room and shut the door. A stainless steel examining table stood in the middle of the room. The room was brightly lit with huge fluorescent tubes overhead. On the wall hung the famous Norman Rockwell print of the doctor about to give a young boy a big needle in his bum.

"Please, have a seat," said Dr. Varley.

"I'll stand," said Gilbert. "I've been driving all day."

"Snow in Parry Sound?"

"Not this time."

"You're lucky."

"Just cold. I hear they have a sauna at the Days Inn."

"Do they?" said Varley, congenially. "I've never been."

"I'm sorry about Cheryl," said Gilbert.

Varley shrugged, raising his eyebrows. "She was too young."

"And about Donna as well."

Varley nodded with grave resignation, as if death were death and there was nothing you could do about it.

Gilbert continued. "You saw her in November?"

Varley looked at him, puzzled. "No," he said. "Who told you that?"

"I thought there was a family meeting."

"What family meeting?"

"Did you not go down to Toronto with Larry in November?"

"No," he said. "No, I was right here, working. I didn't go anywhere in November."

Maybe Matchett had his information wrong. "But Larry went down, didn't he?"

Varley shrugged. "Wasn't it October? I know he went down sometime around then." A slight frown came to the doctor's face. "Is it really that pertinent?"

"I can't seem to find your brother," said Gilbert.

"My brother's at sea right now."

"At sea?"

"He hires on occasionally. I saw him just before he left. He's been at sea since February seventh."

Again Gilbert stared at the doctor. Here was another discrepancy, information that didn't jibe with what Gilbert already knew: Larry Varley, the rented Crown Victoria. Yet there was nothing of a lie in the way Dean Varley spoke; as far as Dean Varley was concerned, this was just a simple statement of fact.

"Are you sure?" asked Gilbert.

Dr. Varley rubbed his hands together and leaned against the examining table. "Look, detective, I know you have to do this. I know you have to check everything out. So I'll make it easy for you. Larry and I had nothing to do with either of those murders. He was in Halifax on the fifth, and at sea on the eighteenth. I was up here, in Sudbury. I know you have to do this, but I think you might be wasting your time."

"And what were you doing on the night of the eighteenth?"

"I went to the Sudbury Wolves hockey game with two friends, Bill Fournier and Kevin Horvath. Linda will give you their numbers. And if that's not enough, a lot of people saw me at the arena. As for Donna's murder, one of your other detectives has already called about it . . . is it Ballantine?"

"Bannatyne."

Varley nodded, still congenial, still cooperative. "I was judging a dog show that day."

"And what about Larry?"

"Like I said, he was in Halifax by that time."

"Getting ready to ship out," said Gilbert, playing along.

"That's right," said Dr. Varley.

"And did he stay in a hotel down there?"

"How would I know?"

"What was the name of his ship?"

"The *Gerald* something," said Varley. "The *Gerald Peyton*. No, wait a minute, the *Gerald Hayden*," he said.

"Did he drive down?"

"He took the bus."

Gilbert raised his eyebrows. "You're sure about that?"

"Larry doesn't have a car."

"Maybe he rented one."

Varley shook his head. "I had to lend him the money for bus fare." Varley stood up, arched his back, and glanced out to the back parking lot. "You know, I wish you'd stay away from Larry. He's had a hard life. He's made some bad choices. And he carries a lot of emotional garbage around with him. He doesn't want to hear about Cheryl. He has a real big problem with her. There's stuff about . . . my dad and Cheryl . . . and Larry really doesn't . . ." Varley's eyes narrowed. "Have you . . . I mean how far have you gone with this?"

"We checked it out," admitted Gilbert. "It was a snowmobile accident, wasn't it?"

"Actually, hypothermia. My father froze to death."

Gilbert felt something loosen inside; a connection made, a mystery illuminated, a piece of the puzzle suddenly fitting. The manner of death. Hypothermia.

"He was injured in the snowmobile accident," explained Dr. Varley. "Cheryl and Donna were with him. The snowmobile was totaled. The girls had to walk five miles. My father couldn't move. By the time help finally arrived he was already dead. Have you ever spent a winter up here, detective?"

"No."

"The day my father died it was minus forty. And this is what Larry doesn't understand. Those girls had to walk five miles to get help. When the temperature's that cold it doesn't take long. My father didn't stand a chance. Larry thinks he did. Especially because the authorities thought the whole thing was confusing enough to have a close look. There's no way Cheryl could have saved my father. Larry thinks otherwise. He was close to Dad. He's never forgiven Cheryl since the inquest."

"Inquest?" said Gilbert.

"There was an inquest into my father's death."

Gilbert took out his notebook. Varley made a face. "I should have kept my mouth shut."

"There'll be a record," said Gilbert.

"I wish you'd stay away from Larry," repeated Varley. "You're just going to open old wounds. He took my father's death badly. He never really got over it. They were like this," said Varley, crossing his fingers. "A lot of people, when someone they love dies, they look around for someone to blame. Cheryl just happened to be the one he decided on. The snowmobile crashes, my father's too injured to move, the girls make a five-mile trek to get help. Cheryl's thirteen, Donna's nine. Both were badly frostbitten by the time they got to the nearest town. The snow was two feet deep in some places. Do you know what it's like trudging through snow like that? Slow going, especially for a couple of scared girls. Cheryl had to keep waiting for Donna. She might have gone ahead, but then what would have happened to Donna? Donna would have frozen to death as well. So that's what I tell Larry. Don't blame Cheryl for Dad's death. Thank her for saving Donna's. I don't know what the authorities found so confusing. And I don't know why Larry won't give it up. But you're not going to help matters if you—"

"I've got to look into the inquest," said Gilbert. A woman poked her head in the door, must have been Charlene, holding a cocker spaniel under her arm, and just as quickly ducked out again when she saw Gilbert and Varley. "Did you ever talk to the authorities about the inquest?"

Varley shrugged. "Not really," he said. "I was away at school and I . . ." He peered up at the ceiling, squinting, trying to recall. "Something about a chest injury not being consistent . . ." He gave it up, looked at Gilbert. "Look, I really don't . . . at least I can't remember. It was twenty-five years ago. There was some sort of investigation and everything was cleared."

Back at the Days Inn, after a swim and a sauna, Gilbert called Lombardo long distance using the squad's calling card and asked him to check the *Gerald Hayden*.

"I don't think it's going to pan out," he said, "not when we have a record of Larry Varley renting the Crown Victoria." The flicker of the TV brightened the room, tuned low to the Weather Channel. "I'm starting to think Larry Varley might be the guy."

Paul Varley, frozen. An inconsistent injury to the chest. Cheryl Latham, frozen. And Cheryl's bullet wound to the chest. The similarities were too striking to ignore.

"Maybe," said Lombardo. "But let's not jump to conclusions. We got the results back on the blood samples from Cheryl's apartment."

"And?"

Out on the road, Gilbert watched an oil truck rumble by. "It's Latham's blood in the kitchen."

Gilbert watched the truck as it turned the corner and disappeared behind a large mound of granite toward Ramsey Lake. So was all this up in Sudbury a blind alley? The snow was still coming down, not much, but steady. Somehow he couldn't believe that. Not when Larry Varley was supposed to be in the middle of the Atlantic somewhere and was instead riding around in a Crown Victoria.

"Okay, so he's still on our list," said Gilbert. "Have you confronted him?"

"Not yet." He heard Lombardo rustle some paper on the other end of the line. "I like to go in with a lot of evidence. Speaking of which, we got the toxicology results back as well."

"And?"

"It's a kicker." Gilbert heard the papers rustle again. "They found high levels of something called Kedamine."

"Kedamine?" said Gilbert. "What the hell is Kedamine?"

"It's an animal tranquilizer," said Lombardo. "Veterinarians use it to calm excitable animals. I guess Cheryl had enough in her bloodstream to put her right out."

Dr. Dean Varley. Veterinarian. Gilbert looked at his french fries, not hungry anymore. Maybe Sudbury wasn't a blind alley after all.

Chapter Eleven

On the last day of February, the skies cleared as a fierce north wind blew through Sudbury. The temperature dropped, and, with the windchill, hovered somewhere around minus 37 Celsius. Gilbert sat in the coffee room of Sudbury Regional Police Headquarters, his hands around a warm cup of coffee. Uniforms looked at him curiously. Some nodded a greeting. Others sat at tables in groups, some speaking French, others English. Not much crime in Sudbury. Last night, they had a couple of break-ins, an auto-theft, and an Ojibwa Indian frozen to death in a snowbank clutching a bottle of White Satin. Reminded him of Toronto back in the seventies.

Guy Faucher came in holding a sheet of paper. He sat down, not looking too pleased.

"They can't find it in the Sudbury office," he said. "The case is old. After a while they send them out to storage."

"They have nothing on computer?"

"Nothing before 1979."

"Then where is it?" asked Gilbert.

"It might be in Ottawa, at the Solicitor General's Office. They have a huge storage facility there. Or it could be in Toronto. They're going to check."

"How long will it take?" Gilbert again thought of Lombardo, how he might lose his job if he didn't get a decent collar on the Latham case. "We're under a little pressure."

"The girl said anywhere from three weeks to six months."

"That long?"

"Sometimes it takes a year. I guess a subpoena might hurry things along, but not by much." Faucher slid the piece of paper across the table. "I thought this might help. It turns out we did our own investigation."

Gilbert looked at the sheet of paper. A suspicious death report, recounting the details of Paul Varley's death. A scrawl in the Extra Remarks section: foul play hasn't been ruled out. Signed by a Detective Harry Blair, dated February 1971.

He followed Elm Street out past Big Nickel Road onto Route 144 into the Onaping Falls Region, where the road twisted through rock, up and down, hairpinning, coiling past old slag heaps and blackened outcroppings.

After ten miles, the bush, now far away from the sulfuric emissions, began to come back. The road sometimes dipped low through bog and marsh, where the reeds stuck up brown through the ice, and where dead spruce and birch, unable to support themselves past a certain height in the thin layer of rock-clinging soil, lay upended on frozen shores in a tangle of stumps and roots. He continued past an abandoned maple sugar bush, took a side road around a derelict mine shaft, where the corrugated steel on the head frame was practically rusted through, and finally came to a mailbox that said Blair along the bottom, lacquered pine with the letters burned right in, and a design of mallard ducks taking off up the side. Here he found a small private lane.

He drove along the private lane through a stand of copper birch, up over a hill, then down a steep grade. At the bottom, shaded by huge spruce trees, he saw a grey GMC pickup truck parked next to a log barrier. The log barrier had a dead-end sign nailed to it. He parked beside the pickup and got out of his car. So cold outside, he immediately coughed. He looked beyond the log barrier where he saw a marsh, frozen solid; beyond the marsh, a large rocky hill; and perched in and amongst the cedar and birch on the hill was a small two-storey home with smoke coming from the chimney. A low walkway extended out over the marsh, really a bridge leading to the hill the home was on. Gilbert mounted the steps and crossed the walkway. The walkway skirted the edge of a seventy-five-foot-long beaver dam; to the right the water was three feet higher than the water to the left, pinned in by the dam. He didn't know beavers made dams that long; this was more a dike. Up ahead he heard a dog barking. In a moment a black and tan mongrel appeared. The dog trotted out over the walkway, stopped a few yards away, and continued to bark at Gilbert, not viciously, more in excitement.

"All right, Sandy, that's enough now."

Gilbert looked up. A man appeared at the end of the walkway, about seventy years old, dressed from head to foot in a blue snowsuit, a little Ski-Doo logo above the breast pocket, a blue tuque with little red maple leafs on it pulled down over his head.

"She won't bite you," said the man. "We don't get that much company out here. She's a little excited." The man peered at him quizzically. "You're Detective Gilbert?"

Gilbert nodded. "I'm glad you could see me at such short notice. Harry Blair?"

"That's what my mother called me."

He was tall, barrel-chested, a rugged-looking man with a handlebar mustache and a large forthright nose. Gilbert was six-one; Blair had at least four inches on him.

"We might as well get you out of this cold," said Blair, giving a cursory glance at Gilbert's thin coat. "You're not dressed for it. Betty's not here right now, she works part-time at the A&P, but I've got some coffee brewing and I've baked a half dozen biscuits. You'll like my biscuits. They're great with maple syrup. Or eat them just plain if you like."

Gilbert followed Blair the rest of the way across the walkway and up the hill. Sandy now nuzzled experimentally at his hand, no longer barking, tail wagging frantically.

"A nice place you got here," said Gilbert.

"I think so," said Blair. "I've had enough of town. So has Betty."

The house itself was actually constructed of logs. Three cats sat in the living room window staring down at them. A snowmobile was parked around the side. Wood chips littered the snow near the front steps, where there was an axe, a chopping block, and small pile of firewood. If it weren't for the huge radar dish on the roof, Gilbert might have convinced himself he'd just stepped into the nineteenth century.

They climbed the steps. Blair opened the door and they went inside. The air smelled of wood smoke.

"You can hang your coat up there," said Blair. "Here's the living room. You make yourself comfortable and I'll go get coffee."

"Thanks."

Blair kicked off his mukluks, pulled off his snowsuit, and disappeared down the hall to the kitchen, the three cats following him. Gilbert hung up his coat and sat in the comfy green armchair by the fire. The coffee table was made from a single cross-section from the trunk of a large tree and the walls were panelled with cedar. A pipe, a pouch of pipe tobacco, and a spin-top ashtray sat on the table. Above the fireplace there hung a pair of moose antlers. A Blue Jays pennant hung from one of the antlers. Maybe someday he and Regina would retire like this. He could do without the antlers but he had no objection to cedar panelling. And the view of the marsh was soothing.

Blair came in with a tray of coffee and biscuits, and a litre tin of maple syrup. He set the tray on the table and eased himself into the other chair, grunting with the effort.

"There we go," he said.

Gilbert opened his briefcase and took out a mimeographed copy of Blair's decades-old report on the Paul Varley death.

"There it is," he said.

Blair lifted the report and glanced at it.

"I was never a star when it came to cursive penmanship," he said. He slid the report on the table. "I can hardly read this. But I remember the case well. Snowmobile accident over by Onaping. Out near Moose Lake. Had a deep snowfall the night before. Must have been twenty-five inches. And bitterly cold. Everything was buried. All the rock rounded over with snow. A lot of wind, too, a lot of drifting." Blair shrugged, lifted a knife, sliced a biscuit in half, drenched it in maple syrup and took a bite. "You have to know your trails. They've marked a lot of them over the last ten years, but back then none of them were marked. Varley went head first into a boulder. I guess it looked like a small hill, with all that snow, and he thought he could take it. Or maybe he was just snow-blind by that time. He went right into it, with the girls in a small trailer hitched to the back."

"So he was thrown forward?" said Gilbert.

"That's what the girls told us. And by the way, I was awfully sorry to hear about Donna and Cheryl. That's really too bad. I hope you catch your man."

Gilbert tapped the report. "Was there any follow-up on this?"

"The inquest was satisfied," said Blair. "Not me. It bugged the hell out of me."

"The inconsistent injury to the chest?" said Gilbert.

"That didn't bother me so much," said Blair. He spooned some sugar into his coffee. "It was the one to the head that got me. The one that fractured his skull. He was wearing a helmet, heaven help him. He shouldn't have been injured like that."

Gilbert stared at Blair. He swallowed a few times. "I don't know about the head injury," he said. "I can't get my hands on the coroner's report."

"His forehead," said Blair, tapping his brow. "Varley always rode with his knee on the seat, his foot on the right runner. When he hit the boulder, the snow compacted in front of him, making a bit of a ramp. He was thrown up and over the boulder. His left leg snagged the edge of the windshield, gave his leg a bad twist, but didn't break it. He could have walked out with the help of a stick. But then you have this head injury. Even if he wasn't wearing a helmet, to sustain a head injury like that he would have had to be thrown directly against the boulder. And he wasn't. He was thrown clear of the boulder. He landed in two feet of snow on the other side. Of course, when I finally got there, most of the scene was obliterated. I was hoping to find some evidence in the snow prints. But everybody had walked all over everything. So I took the girls aside one by one. Cheryl stuck with her story. She said he was thrown clear and that she had no idea how he got the head injury. She was cool. But Donna, she's not so bright, and when I asked her about it, she fished around, looking for some explanation, said maybe he hit the boulder after all. I said, are you sure about that? She just started crying. She looked scared. I knew something wasn't adding up. I grew

convinced Cheryl had something to do with it. Even in deep
snow like that they should have reached Onaping in an hour."

"I thought it was five miles," said Gilbert.

"Not if you cross Moose Lake," said Blair, "which Cheryl
should have done. Hell, they'd gone across Moose Lake on
the way out. Why'd she decide to go around on the way
back?"

"Maybe she got scared," suggested Gilbert. "Maybe she
was afraid of thin ice."

"The ice was ten feet thick, mister. She went the long way
around because she wanted to be sure. Took them five hours.
When we finally got out to old Paul Varley his head was
bashed and his helmet was lying on the ground, and he was
frozen to death. You could see right away that the kippers
were nowhere near the kettle, even though Cheryl said
otherwise."

"So that's when they decided on an inquest."

"I brought it to the coroner's attention and he thought we
should go ahead. Not that it did any good. Cheryl was such
a sweet-looking girl. Small, petite, real girl-next-door, and no
one could believe she would bludgeon her stepdad that way.
The boys were real upset. Especially Larry. I guess he must
have been nineteen or twenty at the time. After the inquest,
you could hear him wailing in the hall. He spent a while in
the hospital after that, I don't know whether it's because his
dad died, or if it was something else."

"But the cause of death was hypothermia."

Blair stopped his coffee cup halfway to his lips and stared
at Gilbert. "If you ask me, mister, the cause of death was
Cheryl Varley. She whacked him good and hard and left him
there to freeze. I worked on that case for a year. If something
doesn't add up, it doesn't add up. Sure, the coroner ruled
accidental death, but I didn't believe it then, and I don't

believe it now. She killed him. There's no doubt in my mind. And she as good as ruined Larry Varley's life in the process."

Gilbert took a biscuit and poured a little maple syrup over it. He thought of Cheryl Latham's body lying on the Dominion Malting pier, frozen, legs curled, frost in her hair, the big gunshot wound to her chest. Was it revenge on Larry Varley's part? Was it just coincidence that both stepdad and stepdaughter died of hypothermia, both with significant injuries to the chest, both on a cold day in February? And if so, why now, twenty-five years later? What made Larry Varley come down from Sudbury and kill his stepsister at this particular time? He bit into his biscuit and chewed thoughtfully. Was Cheryl in some way responsible for Donna's murder? And did Donna's murder then trigger Larry's journey south in his rented Crown Victoria? He could see it. Larry Varley somehow stealing Kedamine from his brother's clinic so Cheryl wouldn't struggle, then dumping her in the trunk of his Crown Victoria and taking her down to Cherry Beach. Letting her freeze to death. Then shooting her just to make sure.

"Why would Cheryl want to kill her stepfather?" he asked.

Blair nodded, as if he had anticipated Gilbert's question.

"That's what nobody could understand. I couldn't investigate right away, I got busy, we had a lot of problems that year, the standoff at the Manitouwadge Reserve, with the Indians not letting anybody through, and those two RCMP officers shot to death . . . I got involved in that, they thought I'd be good, I'm half Ojibwa, and the band leaders would listen to me. Had to be June before things settled down. I started with Cheryl's grade-eight teacher at King George Public School, a nice old girl by the name of Violet Brewer. I think she's dead now. Anyway, I spoke to her, and she told me Cheryl was always coming to school with black eyes and bruises. Told me Cheryl was really accident prone, had two broken arms, a dislocated shoulder, a fractured collarbone, even bashed her teeth out once. I'm beginning to think Paul Varley beat her. So I check our own records, and I see he has a record, beat his wife a few times, even spent a couple months in jail. I follow it up with Cheryl's doctor—oh, now, what's his name, Champion I think it was—he's convinced Cheryl's the victim of repeated physical abuse." Blair looked up from his biscuit, his eyes narrowing. "I'd say that's a fairly good motive, if you're beaten within an inch of your life day in and day out by your stepdad."

Gilbert nodded. Cheryl couldn't take it anymore. Her stepdad flew over the windshield and twisted his leg and couldn't get up. She saw the perfect opportunity. She grabbed the nearest rock and beat him senseless. Took a long time getting to Onaping, wanted him to freeze. Talked Donna into going along. And Larry snaps. Larry doesn't know when, he doesn't know how, but he knows he's going to make Cheryl pay.

When he got back to the hotel, he called Lombardo and had him put an all-points-bulletin on Larry Varley's rented Crown Victoria.

"That's a good idea," said Lombardo.

"Why's that?" asked Gilbert.

"Because I did some checking on the *Gerald Hayden*, like you asked?"

"And?"

"The *Gerald Hayden*'s been in drydock for the last two years undergoing repairs," said Lombardo. "Varley's nowhere near that ship."

Chapter Twelve

Gilbert pulled into his driveway on Prestine Heights Boulevard a little after three that afternoon, having made good time on the southbound journey home. He was tired, hungry, thought he'd have a little rest before he went to work, and check up on Nina, who had the day off because of a professional development day at school.

As he entered the foyer, he found Nina sitting halfway up the stairs with a gleeful smile on her face, listening, it seemed, to some noise that was coming from upstairs. Her face was red, and she looked ready to explode with laughter. Gilbert put his briefcase down.

"What's going on?" he said, a crease coming to his brow.

She lifted her finger to her lips. "Shhh," she said. Then she pointed up the stairs, fighting hard to suppress her giggles. "It's Joe and Valerie," she said.

The crease on Gilbert's brow deepened to a frown. "What?" he said.

He took two quick steps across the hall and listened.

He heard the sound of creaking springs coming from the spare bedroom, the telltale rhythm that could mean only one thing. All expression left his face and he grabbed Nina by the arm.

"Come on," he said, his voice flat.

The smile dropped from her face; her father was ruining her fun. "Where are we going?"

"We're going skating," he said. "Grab your skates."

"I don't want to go skating," she said, as her father yanked her into the hall. "I want to listen to this."

"You shouldn't be listening to this," he said. He lifted their skates from the hook. "Here."

"I don't want to go skating."

"We're going skating. Where's your coat?"

"It's upstairs."

"Forget the skating. We'll just go for a drive."

"Where to?"

"Wherever," he said.

A few minutes later they were parked next to Topham Park beside the skating rink.

"Why are we stopping?" asked Nina. "Why don't we go to Eglinton Square? I need a new scarf."

He tapped the steering wheel a few times. "Nina . . ." He felt awkward. "You knew what they were doing?"

"Dad, I wasn't born on Mars."

He gave her a quick sideways glance. "Have you ever . . ." He looked out the window where a father was trying to teach his three-year-old son to skate. "You know, with Jeff, or . . ."

Nina's face settled. "Is this going to be a lecture?"

"No," he said. "No, not at all. Forget what I said. Forget I asked you. It's your business. But if you have, I think fifteen's a little too young, in fact, it's actually against the law . . . and I don't want you to think badly of Joe because—"

"I think Joe's cute."

His breath caught. He looked at her and sighed.

"Nina, what Joe and Valerie are doing up in that room right now—"

"Dad, you don't have to tell me."

"I know, I know," he said, "it's just that I get worried . . . can't a dad get worried . . . it was a lot different when I was a kid . . . there wasn't so much risk . . . they teach you about some of that at school, don't they? Your gym teacher or whatever . . . you know about the risks, don't you?"

"You mean AIDS and stuff like that?"

He nodded. "Yeah."

"Dad, they have a condom-dispensing machine at school."

"They do?"

She shook her head, amazed by her father.

"In the girl's washroom?" he asked.

She nodded.

"Oh," he said, trying to act nonchalantly now. "Then I . . ." He felt his face turning red. "Then I . . . it's just that . . ." He turned down the heat; he was feeling hot. "I would hate to see something bad happen to you, that's all. I just want you to know about . . . you know. And I don't want you to think badly of Joe."

"Why would I think badly of Joe?"

"I don't know, I just . . ." Out on the rink, the father was towing his small son along. "Joe's got to be one of the nicest guys I know. This thing he has, you know, the women and all that, we joke about it at work a lot, but he really cares, he's really sensitive, he's not like, you know . . . he does his best to be really kind, and I know he's always smart about it, I know he always goes into it, you know, he always wears—"

"You have a condom-dispensing machine in Homicide?" she asked.

He frowned. "Not right in Homicide. Carol and Sylvia might get a little . . ."

She leaned over and kissed him on the cheek. "Don't worry, Dad. When the time comes—and the time hasn't come yet—I'm going to be careful. But I think I'm going to wait a while. Jeff and I . . . he's nice, but I . . ."

She glanced out at the skating rink. Two older boys were now passing a puck back and forth.

"It's all right," said Gilbert. He put his hand on the back of her neck and rubbed. "You know what? You're a smart girl."

She shrugged. "I've got smart parents," she said.

Back at the house, Lombardo was waiting for him at the kitchen table with a guilty look on his face. Nina went upstairs. Gilbert soon heard music.

"I saw you drive away with Nina," said Lombardo. "I guess you've figured things out."

Gilbert looked at his partner for a few seconds, then walked to the stove and put the kettle on. "Coffee?" he said.

Lombardo picked up a deck of cards and started shuffling. "Sure," he said.

Gilbert took the kettle to the sink and rinsed it. "You know, you're really supposed to rinse this with vinegar every once in a while," he said. "It gets scaly, have you noticed that?"

"Barry, I'm sorry."

Gilbert filled the kettle with water. "Sorry about what?"

Lombardo stopped shuffling the cards. "You know . . . about . . . don't think I planned it this way. I met her for lunch at the Goethe Institute and I drove her home. And before we knew it—"

"You don't have to explain it to me," he said. "I think I know the mechanics."

Lombardo split the deck and looked at the nine of clubs. "Yeah . . . well . . . I'm sorry, I just—"

"Valerie's leaving on Tuesday, you knew that, didn't you?"

He put the kettle on the stove and turned on the gas burner. Lombardo looked suddenly doleful.

"She's a wonderful girl, Barry."

"I know."

Gilbert came to the table and sat down.

"No, I really mean it, Barry, she's wonderful. I know she's a lot younger than I am, but that doesn't seem to make a difference, we just seem to be . . . I don't know, like we're made for each other, or something. Have you ever met a woman like that, Barry? You can feel it flowing all over you. I honestly think I might . . . I mean if things didn't seem so impossible, if she didn't have to go back to Germany—"

"Don't ask her to marry you," said Gilbert.

Lombardo looked up from his deck of cards. "Why not?"

"Because you'd ruin her life."

Lombardo smirked. "Very funny." He went back to shuffling his cards. "I don't know, she's just so nice, she's so . . . when she walks into a room, you can feel it, this energy. Everybody's looking around, and no one can figure out why suddenly they're having such a good time, and then they see Valerie, and they understand . . . I don't know, Barry, it's her, she does this to people."

"I'll be taking her out to the airport on Tuesday." The kettle began to sing. "You want to come?"

Lombardo looked at Gilbert in surprise. "You're really not mad about this . . . about me being upstairs? You're really okay about it?"

Gilbert felt his face pulling back in an expression of ambivalence. "I just don't like seeing people get hurt."

Lombardo lifted the top card and gazed at it, the king of diamonds. Gilbert contemplated his partner. He hadn't seen Lombardo down like this in a long time. He got up and spooned instant coffee into two cups. He took the kettle off the burner and poured hot water into the mugs. Lombardo was sliding into one of his Piedmontese funks. Nothing he could do. He would just have to weather it. Gilbert put the kettle back on the burner and brought the mugs to the table. Move on. Change the subject.

"Anything happen since I talked to you this morning?" he asked.

Lombardo nodded. "I saw Latham."

Gilbert sat down. "So?"

"He says he was in her apartment the end of January helping her move some stuff. He says when they were cleaning up he cut himself on some broken glass in a garbage bag."

"So he cut himself the end of January, not the eighteenth of February, is that what he's saying?"

Lombardo spooned four sugars into his cup. "I called the Center, had them look at the blood again."

"Yeah?"

"Latham's telling the truth. The blood's old. According to the Center it's about two weeks older than the blood we found in the bathroom, Cheryl's blood. The white cells were denatured. I'm thinking we might have reached a dead-end with Latham."

Gilbert moved the spoon to one side. "Not necessarily," he said.

"Have you talked to Matchett about his gun yet?" asked Lombardo.

Gilbert felt his shoulders stiffening. He turned away, looked out the kitchen window. He felt Lombardo's dark eyes boring into him. How long was he going to put this off? He tapped the table a few times with the end of his spoon. Why did coincidence always have to conspire against Matchett? Finally, he turned back to Lombardo and took a deep breath. This was his dilemma: he wanted to protect his old partner but he didn't want to lie to his current one.

"Look, Joe, there's a problem with Matchett's gun," he said.

"Why?" said Lombardo. "He doesn't want to give it to you?"

"It's not that . . . it's just that he can't give it to me."

"Why not?"

Gilbert felt his face reddening. "Because it's gone. I went over there on Wednesday. I was there just before we had that meeting with Marsh. We go up to his apartment, we open his gun case, and his gun is gone. I didn't want to tell you guys. Alvin's had to put up with a lot of shit and I didn't want to—"

"You mean gone, like stolen, or gone, he got rid of it."

"Just gone. As in, it wasn't there and he didn't know where it was."

"So like it was stolen?"

"I don't know. There was no sign of any forced entry. I don't think it's such a big deal. I mean, come on, Joe, Alvin's one of us."

"Listen to yourself, Barry."

"What? You really think he killed Cheryl Latham?"

"No, but listen to yourself."

"What's there to listen to?"

"You've got to be analytical," said Lombardo. "You're letting old ties get in the way."

"He was my partner for seven years, Joe. I think I know what he's like. He's a good cop."

"I know. But maybe you're not working this lead as hard as you're working some of the others."

"The gun is gone, so what?"

"Yeah, but no forced entry," said Lombardo.

"That could mean anything."

"He's the only one anywhere close to Cheryl who has the right kind of gun. And now the gun is gone. I'm sorry, Barry, but that's a stroke against him. Then I read your Shirley Chan interview, says Matchett had an affair with her, and that's another stroke against him."

"You know, maybe I'm pissed off at you after all."

"Don't get excited," said Lombardo.

"I'm not excited. I just think we have better leads than Alvin. The man drives a Tempo. That's a far cry from a Crown Victoria."

"Okay, okay, then I'm going to tell you another stroke against him, something I found out while you were up north. I've been going through my list, you know me, the librarian, and I got Halycz and Telford to help me, checking out all the Crown Victorias. And guess what? The legislative car pool? They have seven Crown Victorias, all of them midnight blue."

Gilbert felt his lips stiffening and his shoulders sinking. It was like a cold wind was blowing through him. Like he was always trying to believe in something but reality always got in the way. Those seven years with Matchett on patrol, he sometimes longed for those years, when everything seemed straightforward and simple. You reach into your past, you lift it up, and it starts to glow after a while, like a pearl; and each year a new layer of lustre is added. He didn't want to let that go.

"What about Larry Varley's Crown Victoria?" he said. "It's midnight blue, too."

Lombardo shrugged. "Yeah, there's that . . . but I . . . we still have to check out this legislative carpool thing. They probably have a record of who took what car out when," he said.

"So if we see Alvin took a car out the night of the eighteenth, then we take a serious look at him," said Gilbert.

Lombardo shook his head. "We take a serious look at him anyway, Barry. Don't forget the gun."

Gilbert frowned. He tried to be impartial. "There's something else about that gun, Joe. No forced entry, right? Alvin raised the possibility that maybe when he was having friends over, one of his friends could have taken it."

Lombardo shrugged. "So we get a list."

"And then I asked him if somebody had a key. And . . . I don't know . . . he hesitated, got quiet . . . and I could see him thinking about it . . ."

"Shit, Barry."

"I know, I know."

"He hesitated?" said Lombardo.

Gilbert nodded. "He said he was the only one who had a key. Like he was trying to protect someone."

Lombardo looked incredulous. "Shit, Barry," he repeated.

"I wanted to work all these other angles before . . ."

"You should have told me, Barry. I know he saved your life way back when, but I'm your partner now."

Chapter Thirteen

On the first day of March, Saturday, Gilbert once again stood in Cheryl Latham's apartment. On his own time. Working the case outside rotation hours. Because there was one thing they still hadn't figured out. March, and maybe the days were a bit longer, but snow still plummeted from a slate grey sky, batting hard against the panes of Cheryl's living room window, collecting on the sill. Maybe what he was looking for wasn't here; maybe in the perp's gentle and neat toss of her apartment he had found what he had been looking for and had taken it away. But Gilbert didn't think so. The search was too complete. Nothing had been left unchecked. And that was a sure sign of an unsuccessful search.

He stood next to the couch and stared. Rug, bookcases, TV, CD player, Technics turntable, speakers, Eskimo soapstone carvings, love seat, chair, pillows, blinds, birdcage, coffee table, lamps, magazine rack . . . silence seemed to coagulate in thick layers around each object. And in the silence he felt the connections forming. He walked over to the magazine rack and flipped through the magazines and catalogues one more time, looking for something flat, a document that would fit between the pages of a magazine. He grabbed each magazine by the spine and shook. Nothing. The radiator pipes clanked in the walls. He stood up. Listened to the clank fade and the radiators hiss. He stared out at the snow. Did you kill your stepfather, Cheryl? Is that why everything must be so neatly ordered, as if with this precision you hope to obliterate the chaos of that single act? The dead parrot. Gone now, sent to Forensic, but so far devoid of clues; there was no real way they could lift latent fingerprints from feathers. But he was sure that dead parrot meant something.

He stared at the birdcage. And as he stared at it, it seemed to become the only object in the room. Made to look like bamboo, but when he got close he saw that the bamboo was actually made of metal. Cage door open. Newspaper spread out on the cage floor. The connections again began to form. Parrot shit and bird seed all over the newspaper. Yes, Cheryl, I see what you've done. He reached through the cage door and lifted the newspaper. Nothing underneath, just the bare metal floor. He pulled the newspaper out, shaking as much of the seed back into the cage as he could. The newspaper caught on the door frame. As he tugged it free, something slipped from between its pages and fell to the floor.

A zip-lock glassine bag with some papers inside. Documents.

He lifted the bag and pulled out the documents.

Bank statements. From the Bank of the Bahamas. Freeport, Grand Bahama Island. The Xanadu Beach Branch. He scanned quickly for the account-holder's name. Scuba-Tex Ltd., a division of Ontario Corporation 601847. He looked at the balance. $247,662.02. Nearly a quarter million dollars. He could only begin to guess what this meant. But he knew he had a major clue.

Lombardo was working overtime on the case too. Gilbert found him downtown at headquarters and showed him the document.

Lombardo looked up at him. "Ontario Corporation 601847," he said. "That's Latham's corporation. Remember I checked it out when I was looking into Danny's Crown Victoria."

Gilbert felt his blood quickening. "So Latham's still in the running?" he said.

Lombardo shrugged. "I guess so."

Gord and Diane Danby, Donna Varley's downstairs neighbors on Crawford Street, returned from their Florida vacation Sunday afternoon. Bob Bannatyne and Gilbert interviewed them that evening.

"She was shot on the fifth," said Bannatyne. "I know I've already gone over this with you, but we want to go over it again. You left for your vacation on the sixth. The body was discovered by your friend, Natalie Carels, when she came over on the evening of the seventh to water your plants and collect your mail. I took your statement over the phone on the seventh." Bannatyne glanced down at his notes. "I just want to make sure we have this all straight."

Gord and Diane nodded. "We called up the stairs on the morning of the sixth to say good-bye," said Diane. "Not that we knew her that well. She stayed to herself most of the time. We got no answer so we just thought she was out."

Gord spoke up. "To tell you the truth, we were a little nervous about leaving her here," said Gord. "There's no private entrance. Not that we have a lot of valuables, but, you know, she didn't look . . . she really wasn't our kind of person. We have a lock on our living room door, and we put a lot of stuff in there."

Bannatyne nodded. "I hope I didn't ruin your vacation," he said.

Diane glanced out the window at the snow, which was coming down steadily. "I don't know if I want to live here now," she said forlornly.

Bannatyne sighed sympathetically. "I know what you mean," he said. "Murder can really wreck a place."

Gord put his hand on Diane's arm. "It's all right," he said.

"Who gave the statement?" asked Gilbert. He turned to Bannatyne. "Or did they both give a statement?"

"I gave the statement," said Diane. "Gord was on a fishing charter."

"So let's just go over it for Detective Gilbert's sake," said Bannatyne. He looked at Diane. "On the evening of the fifth you stayed late at the office because you wanted to finish all your outstanding work before you went on vacation." Diane nodded. Bannatyne turned to Gilbert. "We verified that. She was there. The security guard saw her and so did one of the dictaphone typists. Gord, you were here all night except for that hour you had to go to your travel agent to make some last-minute changes in your plans. That was from about eight-thirty to nine-thirty. Correct?"

Gord nodded. "Correct."

"And when you left, Donna's TV was on, and when you came back, Donna's TV was off."

"That's right."

He turned to Gilbert. "We had officers in Florida check for residue on Gord's hands. He was clean. And we checked with his travel agent. He was there. We figure the murder took place in the hour he was away."

Gilbert nodded. "Okay."

Bannatyne looked at Diane. "Diane, you told me Larry Varley stayed with Donna in November, was away for December, and came back in January."

"Yes."

"But you never heard them fighting."

"No."

"And Donna never said anything that would lead you to believe that there was any friction between them."

"Other than telling us he was her brother, she didn't say anything about him. They seemed to get along. They were quiet. They watched a lot of TV."

Gilbert interrupted. He looked at Gord. "You said you had to go to your travel agent on the evening of the fifth. What kind of change did you have to make?"

Gord Danby looked at him, his eyes narrowing. "Not really a change, actually. We won some concert tickets. At least that's what they said. When I got there, no one knew what I was talking about."

Gilbert and Bannatyne looked at each other. Then Bannatyne turned to Diane. "That wasn't in your statement," he said.

A knit came to her brow. "I guess I forgot about it," she said. "Is it important?"

Gilbert looked at Gord. "Was it just a mix-up?"

"That's what they said," replied Gord. "They have two new guys working there."

"But did you verify it?" asked Gilbert.

"I was in Florida the next day," said Gord. "It was the farthest thing from my mind."

"So it wasn't your regular travel agent who phoned you then?" asked Gilbert.

"No."

"Who was it?"

"I guess one of the new guys."

Gilbert glanced at Bannatyne. Get the Danbys out of the house. Use the concert tickets as a pretext. Kill Donna Varley, no witnesses. He turned back to Gord.

"If I played you a tape, would you be able to recognize the man's voice?" said Gilbert.

Gord nodded tentatively. "I think so," he said.

When Gilbert and Bannatyne were out in the car together, Gilbert took a manila folder out of his accordion-style briefcase.

"That was good, Barry," said Bannatyne. Bannatyne started the car and turned the heat on full. "It's colder than a pig's tit," he said. "I'm glad I'm in the Bahamas this Friday."

"Actually, I wanted to talk to you about that," said Gilbert. He reached up and flicked on the overhead light. "You're going to be in Freeport?"

"I already told you," said Bannatyne. "The place is called Pimento Beach. A little resort about eight miles up the coast from Freeport."

Gilbert opened the file folder. "I'm just wondering . . ." Some photographs fell on the floor and he picked them up. "These are shots from Cheryl's funeral. All our major suspects. Latham, Matchett, Danny, Sally. Here's Tom Webb and his secretary, Jane Ireland, too, just in case. You can pull Larry's photo from Donna's file. Do you plan on going into Freeport at all?"

Bannatyne was looking at him suspiciously now. "What the hell are you getting at?"

Gilbert showed Bannatyne photocopies of the bank statements he found in the birdcage and outlined how they might be related to the Latham case.

"I'm just wondering if you can check this out when you're down there."

"You mean like do actual police work while I'm on vacation?"

He was being facetious.

"Yeah," said Gilbert.

Bannatyne looked through the photographs then studied the bank statements. "That's a pile of loot," he said.

"Maybe you might buy one of the bank employees a drink. Ling's okayed some expediency money for the Latham case. Maybe one of the employees might be able to see around the confidentiality rules."

Bannatyne nodded. "Show the employee the photographs, see if he or she recognizes any of them." Bannatyne looked skeptical. "It's a bit of a long shot, Barry."

"Maybe not. Webb goes down to the Bahamas regularly. He has a huge catamaran down there. And Latham has this place, Scuba-Tex. They have an outlet down there."

Bannatyne again looked at the photographs. "I don't know," he said. "They probably have an agent banking for them."

"Maybe," said Gilbert. "But even that might yield some information."

Monday morning. Like Antarctica outside, with wind and snow and killing temperatures, the coldest March 3 on record. But inside the new building they had the heat way up. The detectives, officers, and secretaries fanned themselves with whatever paper, folder, or envelope came to hand. Some rolled up shirtsleeves and loosened neckties. Lombardo's turn for coffee. Gilbert was reading a small story on page five by Ronald Roffey, how the Cheryl Latham case had stalled. He felt his mood diving. Lombardo came in with a couple of extra-large cappuccinos.

"Roffey always makes Monday morning so enjoyable," said Gilbert.

"Christ, do you believe this?" said Lombardo, looking out the window as he took his scarf off. "March third, for Christ's sake."

"You and Valerie had a nice time last night?"

"She hates this weather."

"Is Frankfurt so much warmer?"

"March third in Frankfurt you at least have crocuses. Look at that snow." Lombardo shrugged hopefully. "Maybe they'll have to cancel her flight tomorrow."

"They can fly planes through snow, Lombardo."

"What about ice on the wings?"

"It's supposed to thaw tomorrow."

Lombardo shook his head. "God, I'm going to miss her. This is ridiculous, isn't it? She's a nineteen-year-old kid."

Gilbert grinned as he took his cappuccino from the tray. "So that makes you about two years younger."

"No, I'm serious Barry. I'm going to take a week this July and go to Piedmont. I'm going to drive up and visit her. Her folks own a pig farm."

"So you'll be right at home."

Lombardo laughed. "A little Roffey goes a long way with you."

"I'll be bitter for the rest of the week," he said.

Lombardo shook his head, his eyes growing meditative. "I don't know," he said. "I have a feeling we're going to solve it this week."

"Here comes your Gypsy blood," said Gilbert. "We'll have Building Services put up a special shelf for your crystal ball."

"I don't use a crystal ball," said Lombardo. "I use tarot cards. More murders are solved using tarot cards." He looked at Gilbert quizzically. "I thought you knew."

Carol Reid came down the aisle to his desk, weaving her way around the modular office furniture. She cast an anxious glance toward Marsh's private office. She had a piece of paper in her hand.

"I thought you'd better see this," she said, addressing Lombardo. "Don't let Marsh know. He'd have my gizzard."

She handed the piece of paper to Joe.

"What is it?" asked Gilbert.

"It's Bill's proposed discharge list," said Carol. "He's got to send it to Ling to get the okay for his layoffs."

Gilbert looked at Lombardo. Lombardo's brow settled and his lips squeezed together in a thin line. His dark eyes seemed to glitter like the edge of a sharp knife as he went over the list a second time.

"Shit!" he said. He tossed the list on Gilbert's desk. "What an asshole." He pounded the top of the filing cabinet with his fist. "I could name ten detectives who don't do half the work I do."

Gilbert scanned the list quickly. And suddenly, solving Cheryl Latham's murder took on an even greater urgency. Lombardo's name was right at the top. He glanced at Carol. She was staring at Joe with motherly commiseration. Lombardo walked to the window, raised his elbow against the frame, and looked out at the police courtyard below, where there was another strange statue, a policewoman laying bricks with a mason's trowel. Lombardo was wrapped in lethal silence.

"Don't worry, Joe," he said. "I'll take it to Ling personally if I have to." The phone rang. "We'll have to work round the clock on this Latham case. If we get a collar by the end of the week, I'll have something to take to Ling."

He lifted the phone. "Homicide, Detective Gilbert," he said. The voice on the other end of the line asked for Joe.

"It's for you," he said, handing the phone to Lombardo.

Lombardo pressed the receiver to his ear. "Lombardo here," he said.

Carol stepped forward and lifted the list from Gilbert's desk. "I think I better get rid of this before Marsh walks by," she said.

"Thanks, Carol."

She gave Gilbert a conspiratorial nod and left.

He looked up at Joe. The murderous look had disappeared from the young detective's eyes, and if his brow hadn't yet lifted, he at least had the beginnings of a grin on his face.

"*Molto grazie, signore*," he said to the obviously Italian person on the other end of the line. "*Lei è molto gentile*."

He put the receiver down.

"Who was that?" said Gilbert.

Lombardo's grin was getting broader. "The clerk from the legislative carpool," he said. "He checked the records for the eighteenth." Lombardo jangled his keys in his pocket. "The only person who took out a Crown Victoria on the night of the eighteenth was Jane Ireland."

Chapter Fourteen

Gilbert met Matchett for lunch that day in a small Indian Restaurant, the Raj-Shala, on Baldwin street, just behind Mount Sinai Hospital. They loaded their plates with biryani, bindi bhaji, raita, and chicken tandoori at the all-you-can-eat buffet, ordered a couple of Heinekens, and found a secluded booth at the back in the smoking section under a small brass statue of Shiva. The place was crowded with nurses and doctors. The walls were papered with red velveteen wallpaper, and sitar music filtered from small speakers up in the corner.

"I can tell by the look in your eyes that this isn't a friendly get-together," said Matchett.

Gilbert lifted a chapati and broke it in half. "Here comes our Nan bread," he said. "They really make it . . . some of the other places, they use too much oil. But here they . . ."

The waiter made a space on the table, put the plate of Nan bread down, looked inquiringly at their Heinekens, saw that both were full, filled up their water glasses, and retreated to the kitchen.

"More about Cheryl," said Matchett. "Am I right?"

A disingenuous grin came to Gilbert's face. "Would you mind?"

"As long as you're not here to cuff me."

Gilbert laughed. "Would I buy you lunch only to cuff you? I'm not that generous."

"Look, if it's about my gun, I've reported it. A Detective Spauls is looking into it. Do you know him?"

"Graham? Sure I know him. He's a good man. If anyone can find your gun, he can." Gilbert leaned forward and took a sip of his beer. "No, I just . . ." A waiter walked by with a tray of milk sweets. "I'm not sure you're going to like this line of enquiry."

"I just want to get to the bottom of this, Barry. I hate this. Being a suspect. I just want my name cleared."

"Actually, I wanted to talk about Jane, if you don't mind."

"Jane?" he said. "Jane Ireland?"

Gilbert nodded. "I mean if you'd rather . . . we're just looking . . . you said she took it hard when you and Cheryl . . . you know . . ."

His old partner glanced up at the statue of Shiva, his eyes suddenly apprehensive, and he rubbed his hands together, as if they'd grown cold. Then he turned to Gilbert and he looked like he was on the brink of saying something but at the last moment decided against it.

"Obviously you have something that implicates Jane, or you wouldn't be . . ." He lifted his hand to his face and rubbed the bridge of his nose between his thumb and forefinger, squinting. "Jane's a kind, gracious, thoughtful . . . I really don't think . . . and, yes, she took it hard, but I don't think she snapped. I don't think she took it to the extreme you're suggesting."

Gilbert stared at his friend and took a deep breath. "Alvin, we've always been honest with each other. We've trusted each other. We weren't only partners, we were friends. And still are, I hope. I know it's been a long time, and we both might have changed, but I still think I know you well enough . . . and I might be getting this wrong . . . but something's not . . . I have this feeling—"

"Barry, I don't think Jane killed Cheryl. Didn't you tell me the body was muscled down the stairs and out the laundry room window at the Glenarden, then across the parking lot and into the trunk of a car? Do you think a woman could do that, especially when the body was wrapped up in that carpet?"

Gilbert shrugged. "Jane can bench-press upwards of two-hundred-and-fifty pounds. She spends an hour every evening weight training. That's what you told me."

Matchett stared at Gilbert. He looked like a man who had just been checkmated. "I guess . . ."

"Alvin, you were serious with Jane, weren't you?"

He looked to one side, his lips twisting. "Cheryl was a mistake," he said.

"You loved Jane, you probably still do, and if Cheryl hadn't come along you might have been back together with Jane by this time."

"Cheryl was just something I had to go through," said Matchett. "I got caught up in it, that's all."

"You were drifting away from Jane since June, living half the time at her place and the other half at yours." Gilbert lifted his chin, studying the minutiae of Matchett's expression. "And maybe she lived some of the time over at your place."

"You're right, I don't like this line of enquiry."

"Alvin, we know she has a key."

Matchett's eyes narrowed. "She hasn't got a key."

"You aren't helping her by saying that. We have other evidence that implicates her, I'm not at liberty to say what, but we do. You know what it's like, Alvin, you were a cop. This is staring me right in the face. No forced entry. She knew you had a gun. She knew where to look for that gun. I've already asked at your gun club. They've seen her up at the range."

"Yes, but she doesn't know the first thing about guns."

"What do you have to know? You pull the trigger. You don't need a physics degree. Help me out, Alvin."

Matchett looked up at the statue of Shiva. "I know what you're doing, Barry." He turned away from the statue and stared at Gilbert. "You're trying to get enough probable cause for the duty judge."

Gilbert sighed. He was still trying to protect her, and that could mean charges.

"I have probable cause already, Alvin. I can take what I have to Corning or Wolfe, or any of those guys, and I'll have my search warrant."

"What difference does it make whether she has a key or not?"

"Because if it turns out she does, and you're trying to hide it from me, I'll have to arrest you for obstruction. You see what I'm doing, Alvin? I'm trying to protect you, the same way you're trying to protect Jane. I'm looking out for you, the same way I did on patrol. I know what you went through with the Dennison thing. I don't want you to go through that again. But if it turns out you're obstructing on this murder charge, you might as well say good-bye to . . . you know, your job and everything else."

Matchett's eyes drifted to a stack of ornate stainless steel serving dishes on a table behind the booth to the right. He was fighting with himself. He again rubbed the bridge of his nose, keeping his head turned, his long narrow face creasing in apprehension.

"I guess it doesn't make any difference," he finally said. "I know she didn't do it."

"Then she has a key?" asked Gilbert.

Matchett lifted his Heineken and had a long swallow, contemplating Gilbert over the rim of his glass. He put the glass down and wiped the foam from his lips with the red linen napkin.

"She has a key," he said.

Jane Ireland wasn't home when her landlord opened the door for Gilbert, Lombardo and the rest of the search team. The search warrant stipulated any time, day or night; so they chose Tuesday morning, two weeks to the day Cheryl was found dead.

Gilbert stood in the bedroom while Lombardo and the others methodically combed the rest of the spacious apartment. Directly across the street he saw Winston Churchill Park; to the south, a bit of the main turret of Casa Loma; to the north, St. Clair Avenue, where a red and white streetcar rumbled by. The sky was patchy with clouds, and for the first time since December the temperature had risen above the freezing mark. A robin landed in the bare maple branch outside the window, looked at Gilbert in perplexity, then dipped away toward the ravine, where the massed trees showed up grey against the snow. He shook his head. Patterns were emerging. And he didn't feel particularly good about them. He turned from the window and looked at Jane's dresser. A murder investigation was something you could never entirely control. There were never any tidy endings. And now he couldn't stop the feeling that he was being manipulated. He took a glassine bag and a pair of tweezers out of his pocket, plucked a few hairs from Jane's brush, and put them in the bag. Each step he took now seemed choreographed.

He turned around and studied her bedroom. Rose-colored broadloom covered the floor. A dozen kinds of vitamins crowded the top of her dresser. She had one of those beds with the big brass head-rails. A photograph, enlarged, of Jane and a few other body builders at a weight-lifting competition hung on the wall. What made a woman do that to her body? He took a closer look a Jane in her slinky bikini. Her muscles bulged, her veins stuck out, she was so tanned she could have been black, and she was slick with oil. Where was the aesthetic? He decided he liked Regina's body, soft, a bit plump, now that she was nearing fifty, but still with that pleasing hourglass shape. Making love to Jane would be like making love to a steel girder.

He walked over to the closet and pulled open the louvered door. Power suits and silk blouses, the kind of clothes one would expect. Then a space, then a lot of Matchett's shirts; at least he presumed they were Matchett's. He looked to the floor of the closet. And he paused. A pair of men's winter boots, black Sorels with laces, sat on the broadloom. Matchett's boots, but here in Jane's apartment. He lifted one of the boots, turned it over, and looked at the tread. A series of Greek-keys with cross-lines throughout. He knew he had a match, that this was the boot that made the print in the snow down at Cherry Beach. But why would Jane wear a pair of men's snow boots? He lifted a pair of her half-inch heels from the shoe rack and held the boot and shoe sole to sole. The boot wasn't that much larger. Jane had big feet, Matchett had small. And maybe she realized she was going to leave prints so wore the Sorels as a precaution. But if she was going to be that careful, wouldn't she be careful enough to get rid of the boots afterwards?

He put the boot down and walked out to the living room. Roger Pembleton, from the Forensic Identification Unit, had lifted the pillows from the couch and was reaching down behind. He pulled out a quarter and a penny and put them on the coffee table.

"I've got a pair of men's boots, size-nine Sorels, that have to be boxed in the bedroom," he said. "Anything out here at all?"

"Nothing yet," said Roger. "I don't think she's here a whole hell of a lot."

Gilbert nodded. He looked around the living room, at the rowing machine, the treadmill, the exercise bicycle and the weights. He walked over to the bench, lay down on his back, and tried to press the barbell. He lifted it, but only with some effort.

He was lowering it to his chest a second time when Lombardo strode down the hall from a back room holding a glassine bag in front of him.

"Careful, Barry," he said. "You're going to burst a blood vessel." He held up the glassine bag. "Look what Douglas found."

A .45 caliber round in the bag. And again Gilbert paused. He pressed the barbell back toward the brace, holding his breath with effort, and sat up.

"I got to get to the gym more," he said.

"You know what your problem is?" said Lombardo. "You're all wire and no muscle. You're all sticks, my friend."

Gilbert took the bullet and had a closer look at it.

"It's a soft-nose, isn't it?"

"Same as Donna and Cheryl."

Gilbert stood up and gave the bag back to Lombardo. "Why would she kill Donna?"

Lombardo shrugged. "We don't know that she did."

"Where did Douglas find this?" asked Gilbert, nodding toward the bag.

"Follow me and I'll show you."

Lombardo led him down the hall to a small room at the end. Ken Douglas was carefully going through desk drawers. A ten-year-old PC, a Club American IBM clone, sat on top of the desk. Some old five-and-a-quarter floppies sat in a rack beside it.

"We'll take the disks. We'll download anything she has on her hard drive," said Gilbert. "See if we can find anything about the money."

"I can do that," said Lombardo. "She's got a fresh pack up there."

"Okay."

"Ken, could you tell Barry where you found the .45 round."

"Sure," said Ken. The big man walked around the side of the desk and lifted the edge of the broadloom behind a filing cabinet. "Right here. Wedged between the edge of the carpet and the quarter-round."

Gilbert stared at the spot. He tried to piece it together, how the bullet came to be wedged in that exact spot, behind the filing cabinet, so even if Jane were cleaning in here she probably wouldn't see it, but he couldn't come up with a plausible scenario.

"What's wrong?" said Lombardo.

Gilbert shook his head. "I don't know." He nodded at Douglas. "Thanks, buddy." He slid his hands into the pockets of his coat and looked at Lombardo. Douglas went back to the desk. "I'll be interested to see if we get a match on the hair."

"Come on, Barry, we've got her. You know we're going to get a match on the bullet."

"I guess no sign of the gun."

"No."

"Or any other ammunition."

"She was careful."

"I found the boots," said Gilbert.

"You did?"

"They're Matchett's boots but they were in her closet."

Lombardo's eyes lit up. "Then what more do we need, Barry? We've got her."

Gilbert shook his head. "Still too many variables to call it a game, Joe. What about the money? What about Latham and Scuba-Tex. And where the hell is Larry Varley? And how's it all tie in with Donna's murder?"

Lombardo pressed his lips together. "We get the car this afternoon. Corning's given us the go-ahead. Landry's towing it to the garage at two. When we find Jane's prints on the rearview mirror—"

"She wore gloves, Joe. Remember how cold it was that night?"

"Okay, so what if we find a soil match in the trunk?"

"They probably clean those cars every week."

"We'll go microscopic."

"And how long will that take?"

"I'll break arms if I have to."

Gilbert frowned. "Joe, you're desperate."

"My fuckin' job's on the line, Barry. We need to make an arrest."

Gilbert looked out the window. Another robin, or was it the same one he saw before?

"We're not ready, Joe." He rubbed his hand through his hair. "I see a few pieces, but I don't see the whole picture."

Gilbert and Lombardo took the elevator down to the underground parking garage. At this time of the year, with the roads slushy and loaded with salt, no one much bothered to get their car washed. Toronto streets were always full of filthy cars at this time of the year. But the government Crown Victoria was spotless, immaculate, gleaming.

"Where do we start?" said Lombardo.

"Let's open the trunk," said Gilbert. "I'm sure they've vacuumed, but it's worth a try. Did you find out who returned the car on the morning of the eighteenth?"

"There was no one on duty. If you bring a car in after hours you just leave it there and slip the keys in the box."

"So no one saw anybody."

"Right."

Gilbert nodded. "Figures."

Lombardo took out the keys and opened the trunk. Midnight blue carpeting lined the trunk. As Gilbert had predicted, the trunk, at least to the naked eye, was as immaculate as the rest of the car.

"I guess we'll have to get Roger down here with his clippers and filter vacuum."

Gilbert climbed into the trunk. Lombardo looked at him as if he'd gone crazy. "What the hell are you doing?" he asked.

Gilbert lay on his side, curling his legs, fitting his tall form as best he could. "Remember the gash Cheryl had on the side of her hand?"

"Sure. Where somebody bit her."

"I think she bit herself." Gilbert manuevered right to the back of the trunk. He looked up. There it was, a huge smear of blood, next to the hinge of the trunk, hidden, where no one would ever look. Smart girl. He moved aside. "Get in here," he said. "Take a look at this."

"You want me to get in there with you?" said Lombardo. "Gee, Barry, I think we should stop meeting this way."

"Get in here, you schmuck."

Lombardo got in the trunk and angled up next to Gilbert.

"You see that?" said Gilbert. "She knew she was on the way out. She knew they probably cleaned these cars, and she wanted to leave evidence. So she bit her hand and smeared it up there."

Lombardo stared at the blood smear thoughtfully. "So this is the car."

"We'll have to get the blood tested. You never know. We still have Larry Varley's Crown Victoria to worry about. That blood could be somebody else's but I doubt it."

"So what about Jane?"

Gilbert took a deep breath. "I'm not sure about Jane." He felt heavy with the gravity of what he was about to suggest. "I actually think we should take a closer look at Tom Webb."

Chapter Fifteen

erminal 1. Lester B. Pearson International Airport.
Five o'clock and, wonder of wonders, there was still
light in the sky. What a difference a few weeks made!

Gilbert sat in one of the hard plastic chairs. Lombardo and
Valerie stood in the slow-moving lineup, edging in fits and
starts toward the security checkpoint, where guards scanned
passengers for Lufthansa Flight 403 direct to Frankfurt with
metal-detecting wands, and herded carry-on luggage through
the X-ray unit. Gilbert watched Lombardo. Joe couldn't
smile. All this time Gilbert had been worried that Valerie
would be the one with the broken heart at the end of it all.
But Valerie was bright, cheerful, doing everything she could
to cajole Lombardo. She cupped his chin in her hand and tried
to lift his head, but Joe wouldn't lift his head. Valerie was
going home happy, with no regrets, glad to have her fun with
Joe, but just as glad to say good-bye. The line moved forward.
They were nearly at the barrier. And now he saw Lombardo
pleading with her.

Joe raised his hands in a gesture of entreaty, fingers extended, palms uplifted. Valerie shook her head, patted his shoulder, then . . . then actually pulled out a Kleenex and offered it to Lombardo. The renowned Don Juan of the MTPF was as soft as melted caramel inside. Gilbert looked down at his shoes, salt-stained brown brogues, and shifted in his seat, squirming on Joe's behalf. The women Joe always fell in love with, deeply and truly, were the ones who never worked out. The ones he wanted to marry were the ones who always got away. Gilbert looked up.

They were at the barrier now. Lombardo lifted his arms and hugged her. Tightly. His eyes shut. An expression of exquisite pain on his face. Nineteen years old, a neophyte when it came to matters of love, but she had conquered the Casanova of the Homicide Squad. She looked surprised, even astonished, by the way Lombardo hugged her. But then a look of pity came to her face. She smoothed Joe's rakish mane of dark hair, gave him a kiss on the forehead, disentangled herself from his arms, offered a last few soothing words, backed away, smiling all the time, gave him a final wave, then turned around and disappeared through the security barrier. Joe just stood there, his back to Gilbert, so obviously a cop in his trench coat; stared at the security barrier for nearly a minute then finally turned around.

He looked pale and the rims of his nostrils were red, like he had a bad cold. Only Joe never got colds. Lombardo's face settled and he marched quickly away from the security barrier to the waiting area. Gilbert got to his feet.

"You all right?" asked Gilbert.

Lombardo swallowed a few times, as if he had just eaten something sour, nearly turned to look over his shoulder, but resisted at the last moment. He nodded toward the escalator.

"Let's go," he said.

The two homicide detectives walked through the crowded

terminal toward the escalators. Gilbert put his hand on Lombardo's shoulder and gave it a shake. He didn't say anything. He didn't need to. They were more than partners, they were friends; and everything was understood.

Lombardo's mood lifted considerably when they got back to College Street and found the analysis results from Jane Ireland's apartment waiting for them. The young detective took the reports out of the interoffice envelope and scanned the dot matrix printout.

"What's it say?" asked Gilbert.

"Ballistics matched the bullet to the slugs recovered from both crime scenes," said Lombardo. "A Winchester 230-grain on all three."

"What about the boot?"

Lombardo glanced at the next report. "The tread is identical. They've matched the boot."

"And the hair?"

Lombardo flipped to the next one. "The hair recovered from the suspect's brush is identical to the hair recovered from the victim's sweatshirt. Jane Ireland's hair in both cases." Lombardo put the report down on Gilbert's desk. "Let's go over to the Park. I think Lembeck's working late."

"I don't know, Joe."

"Come on, Barry. You can't be serious."

He shook his head. "I just have a funny feeling about this." He tapped the report. "Roffey's like a wolf on this one. If we screw up now—"

"We need a clearance. It's the only thing that's going to save my job."

"And if you arrest Jane, and she's innocent, that's going to save your job?"

The corners of Lombardo's lips turned downward as his face bunched in a frustrated frown.

"So what do you want? Tell me what you want with this."

Gilbert shrugged. "I want elimination. I want answers to all the outstanding questions. Larry Varley. Latham. Scuba-Tex. The money. Matchett. Donna Varley. Bannatyne's in the Bahamas looking at the money. We've got an APB continent-wide on Larry Varley. I'd say they'll nab him within the next day."

"What are you telling me?" said Lombardo. "You think Jane was framed?"

Gilbert stood up and looked out the window. "Did I tell you yet that Tom Webb does a lot of sailing in and around Freeport?"

Lombardo joined him at the window and they stared at the evening rush hour, a line of cars spilling red glare on the salt-stained pavement.

When Joe next spoke his voice wasn't so strident, nor his tone so insistent. If anything, it was penitential.

"Patience," said Lombardo. "You always tell me that, don't you? And I always forget."

"It's your fiery Mediterranean blood."

Lombardo slid his hands into the back pockets of his sporty pants.

"So the mighty shall fall?" he said.

Gilbert stared down at the statue of the small boy pulling the huge obelisk in his toy wagon.

"I don't know," he said. "But Jane didn't get to be where she is by flying into fits of jealous rage and offing people with stolen weapons. And she didn't get there by leaving a trail of evidence even a blind guy could see."

They got rain the next day. A cold drizzle that seeped into the snow then just sat there. Every street in the city was full of the noise of squelching tires and feet, and passing cars sent up huge curtains of slush onto the sidewalks, often splattering unsuspecting pedestrians. The temperature rose to about plus-2 Celsius and the snow steamed, filling the city with a thin fog. Fender benders tripled. Everybody was in a bad mood because it was so hard to get anywhere.

But up in Gilbert's office, Lombardo's mood was again buoyant. They had the results back from the car pool Crown Victoria. And they were as damning as the results from Jane Ireland's apartment.

"We have her prints on the rearview mirror," said Lombardo. "So she wasn't even wearing gloves. At least not while she was in the car."

"This is what bothers me," said Gilbert. "If she was going to kill someone, why would she leave prints in the car. Why the hell wouldn't she take her own car? Why get one from the legislative car pool, where anyone with an IQ above fifty can look at the log and see who signed it out? I'm sorry, Joe, you've got your refried beans, but I don't see any rice."

Lombardo held up his hand. "Hang on, hang on," he said. "It gets better. They've run the blood at the Center."

"And."

"It's Cheryl's blood."

"So she's the only smart one around here."

"Do you have to be so cynical?"

"My mother accidentally forgot me in the supermarket when I was four. I haven't been the same since."

Lombardo tapped the report. "Look at this here," he said. "They managed to get a sufficient sample for a soil analysis. Distinguishing characteristics. Twenty-three percent bituminous coal. Fourteen percent fermented barley. Just like down at Dominion Malting. Come on, Barry, what do you want?"

"The same as you, Joe," he said. "I want the truth. This is the car, that's the truth. This car has Michelin XGTs. That's true. Cheryl Latham died in the trunk of this car. That might be true. It might not. But let's remember the other truths of this case. A quarter of a million dollars in an off-shore bank account. A dead sister. Even that damn dead parrot. A lot can be gained if we do this one right. But so much more can be lost if we botch it."

Staff Inspector Bill Marsh didn't agree with Gilbert's assessment; since his meeting with Deputy Chief Ling, he'd been on the circulation list for everything and anything to do with the Latham case. Gilbert and Lombardo now sat in Marsh's office, like two miscreant school boys with their principal. Marsh paced in front of his rain-streaked window. Marsh's door was closed, and that was a bad sign.

"You've got the hair," said Marsh. "You've got the boots and the bullet," he said, his patience strained to the limit. "You've got a match on the tire track and the blood and the soil sample. For Christ's sake, Barry, you even have a motive." The big man stopped pacing and pointed at Gilbert. "You should be walking across the street to the Park right now with the papers in your briefcase."

Gilbert went over his reasons one by one: the bank account, Donna, Larry, Latham, even Webb. "And I just don't think Jane would do something like this," he said. "She's not that stupid."

Marsh stood there looking at him. Gilbert was reminded of a bull about to charge.

"You're going to pull a Wesley Rowe on me, aren't you?" said the Staff Inspector.

"No," said Gilbert, "I'm not. I'm just not convinced, that's all."

Marsh slapped the reports with back of his hand. "What more do you need! Someone to tape a sign on her back that says I did it?"

Gilbert glanced at Lombardo. Lombardo stared straight ahead, keeping out of it.

"Have you had a look at the board recently?" continued Marsh. "And have you been reading what that jerk Roffey has been writing in the *Star* about us? What's he going to print when he finds out we have everything we need to write a decent warrant on Jane Ireland. He'll play the Webb angle. He'll write about one justice for those in power, and another justice for the rest of us."

"That's Blatchford," corrected Lombardo, "the columnist. Not Roffey."

"Who the fuck cares?" said Marsh. "The effect is still the same. The public's going to see us as a bunch of incompetents. They're going to say everybody else is doing more for less, why can't Homicide? And Ling's going to flip, and when he flips he's going to shit on me. So how are we going to prevent that?" Marsh's face was turning red. "We're going to fill out our warrant and take it across the street to the Park."

"Bill, look, I . . . if you can just give us a couple more days," said Gilbert.

"You've had two weeks."

"I just don't think Jane did it."

"I want you to arrest her, Barry."

"But you haven't thought it through, Bill," said Gilbert, "not the way Joe and I have." He looked at Lombardo. "Isn't that right, Joe?"

Lombardo looked at Gilbert blankly, like Gilbert was asking him to cut his own throat. "Sure . . . sure," he said, nodding, trying to look dumb.

"What's there to think through?" said Marsh. He stabbed the reports repeatedly with his index finger. "It's all right here. There's enough for an indictment. And ten to one the Crown can convict with it."

"And then we send an innocent woman to prison," said Gilbert, "just like we're doing with Wesley Rowe."

Marsh stared at Gilbert in numb anger. "You always make

me do this, Barry. I got no choice. I try to reason with you. I tell you, look in the mirror, I say that's you, you say it's not you, what the hell am I supposed to do? You say black, I say white. To hell with it. You're going to arrest Jane Ireland. You're going to fill out your warrant and take it across to the Park and have Lembeck or any of those other guys sign it. Then you're going to the legislature and you're going to cuff Jane Ireland and bring her in."

"None of the above," said Gilbert, resolutely. "You'll thank me when you learn I saved your ass."

"I'm not asking you, Barry," said Marsh. "I'm ordering you."

"I'm sorry, Bill, I can't," said Gilbert. "File an insubordination if you want, but I think you're making a big mistake."

Marsh was now livid. His shoulders tensed, making them look even bulkier. He held his arms slightly out from his body, and his chunky fingers were extended, as if they were just itching to strangle Gilbert. He swung like a loaded howitzer toward Lombardo.

"Joe?" he said.

Lombardo stared the Staff Inspector right in the eyes. "Sorry, Bill."

"It's an order, Lombardo."

"Sorry, Bill," he repeated.

The hoods of Marsh's eyes lowered. When he next spoke, his voice was much softer, but twice as deadly.

"Get out," he said. He was calm now. "Get out, the both of you." He shook his head, condemning them as losers. "You're both going to regret this."

Chapter Sixteen

Gilbert finally drifted off to sleep a little past one that morning, having tossed and turned for close to an hour, kept awake by his day of brinkmanship with Marsh. He was just slipping into an uncomfortable dream—another homicide dream, this one with Jane Ireland as victim—when the telephone rang. He let it ring a few times, hoping it would stop, but then Regina shook him and he opened his eyes.

"It's Joe," she said.

He reached for his bedside lamp and turned it on. He shoved himself into a sitting position. "Sorry, Reggie," he said.

She gave him the phone, shrugged, then turned on her side and nestled back into her pillow. Gilbert put the receiver to his ear. He checked his digital alarm clock: 1:47.

"I don't think I asked for a wake-up call," he said to Lombardo.

"They got him. They found him," said Lombardo.

"Who?"

"Larry Varley. The Kingston detachment of the OPP just called. They found him on the Orinoco Reserve, the one that straddles Vermont. He had a trunk full of stolen watches and smuggled cigarettes."

"Shit." Gilbert felt disappointed.

"The Crowfoot Band controls the border there. Indian lands. It's an open gate if the percentages are high enough."

"And stolen watches?"

"I guess he knows someone who rips them off from the factory direct. They're still in their shrink-wrap."

"So where do they have him?"

"Kingston."

"You mean I'm going to have drive out to Kingston now?" said Gilbert.

"I'm going this time," said Lombardo. The rain was still coming down, soaking his bedroom window, one of those early March drenching rains. "I need some time to cool off, anyway."

"Kingston is a nice town. A lot of nice buildings."

"I guess the only one I'll be interested in is the Detention Center. Are you going to work that other angle?"

"Which one?" said Gilbert.

"The Kedamine angle."

"I've already talked to Jack Brett in Burglary. He's going to bring me everything he has."

They were silent. Both knew what the other was thinking. He heard Joe sigh from the other end of the line. "Look, Barry, I'm sorry . . . I know you think . . . but we have to consider . . ."

"Joe, it's a good idea. I agree with you."

Again more silence. Out in the hall, Jennifer went to the bathroom and got a drink of water. "You gave Brett the maps?" said Lombardo.

"I faxed them before I left." Gilbert didn't want to think

about it. It was as much his idea as it was Lombardo's. "Smuggling tobacco, can you believe it?"

"He's a petty criminal. What did you expect?"

"I don't know. I guess I was hoping for a smoking gun."

"This is going to a masterpiece of paperwork. Ling will be able to frame it in his office after it's all over."

"I'm a little worried about Marsh," said Gilbert.

Out in the hall, Jennifer went back to her bedroom. Regina's breathing deepened. And the rain came down steadily.

"Fuck Marsh," said Lombardo.

"Who's our contact in Kingston?"

"A Sergeant Springfield." Lombardo gave him the telephone number.

"And you'll go for background," said Gilbert.

"If there's anything there, I'll find it," said Lombardo.

"Can we be sure he wasn't in Toronto on the night of the eighteenth?" said Gilbert.

"They got him with three stolen credit cards," said Lombardo. "Springfield's already tracking down his purchases. I'm sure we'll find a trail leading south through the States."

By mid-morning, Gilbert had nine burglary files on his desk, all of them animal clinics or veterinarian offices within the target area he had mapped out for Brett the previous day. He immediately eliminated five; stolen property consisted entirely of office equipment: computers, fax machines, and photocopiers. Two others were closed cases; the property stolen had already been recovered. Of the remaining two, one was on the extreme periphery of the target area, at Greenwood and Danforth; drugs were taken, including 600 doses of Keda-mine. But also taken were frozen pedigree collie sperm, three Scotch terrier puppies, and a breeding pair of Siamese cats. As that didn't fit the profile, he was left with the final possibility, the Cabbagetown Animal Clinic, just up the street from the old Winchester Hotel, two-and-a-half blocks from Alvin Matchett's apartment. With bullets, bank accounts, and blood samples, Gilbert found it nearly impossible to believe that the dead parrot would turn out to be the most important clue.

He scanned the Cabbagetown Animal Clinic report a final time. Two thousand doses of Kedamine. In tablet and powder form. What drug traffickers on the West Coast called Special K, the rapist's drug: slip it into her drink and watch her fade into nonresistance. Like Rohypnol, the new one from Europe finding its way to the streets of Miami. Of course, there was no sexual assault in the Cheryl Latham case. But with two thousand doses, Matchett was obviously trafficking the stuff. With two thousand doses, they were bound to find traces somewhere in Matchett's apartment.

He took out the security video from the Glenarden and watched it for the eighteenth time.

Lombardo returned from Kingston that same evening, just after seven. Gilbert was working late as usual, writing up what he hoped would be the last search warrant for the Latham case. Lombardo sat down in the chair opposite Gilbert's desk and stared at Gilbert with bright eyes.

"Elvis is alive," he said, "and being held in Kingston. You should see the sideburns on this guy. And the hair. I swear, Barry, he's in a time warp. Things stopped in 1963 and never moved forward. I didn't know people still used Brylcreem. The guy was covered in tattoos."

"Was he willing to talk?"

"Once we cut him some slack, he was willing to talk about anything."

Lombardo told him first about the credit cards. "He made purchases in Syracuse, New York on the night of the eighteenth. He was nowhere near Cheryl when she was murdered."

"What about background?" asked Gilbert.

Lombardo's eyes widened. "Where do I start?" He leaned forward and rubbed his hand through his hair. "I couldn't stop him. He liked all the attention he was getting. A real boaster. Mainly a petty thief specializing in hotel rooms. He claims he can pick any lock ever made. Even described his tool-kit, said he once worked as a locksmith. That's where he got the credit cards, from hotel rooms." Lombardo glanced anxiously toward the front of the office. "Where's Marsh? I don't see him."

Gilbert shrugged. "I don't know," he said. "He hasn't been in all day."

Lombardo nodded. "You were right, Barry. I think Matchett's our man."

"Varley knew Matchett?"

"Cheryl killed her stephfather," said Lombardo. "At least that's what Varley claims. And he and Donna have been using it as leverage against Cheryl ever since. He says they've been blackmailing her off and on since 1978. He was proud of that. He thought it was a great scam. The fact that Cheryl always paid proves she's guilty. Whenever she ran into the least bit of money, they always came around. When she married Latham a few years ago, they descended like vultures."

Gilbert thought back to the six thousand dollars Latham had told him about. And he thought of Cheryl, everything always in order, trying to make her life neat, trying to make up for the murder of her stepfather. Lombardo continued.

"Varley says Cheryl finally tried to make a deal with them. She would pay them each twenty-five thousand dollars if they agreed to leave her alone for good."

"But didn't Cheryl realize the chances of the murder of her stepfather ever going to trial after all these years was virtually nil."

"Varley says she wasn't so worried about the legal aspects.

She was more worried about her job. She was afraid she might lose her job."

"Did she really believe Donna and Varley would stop after the twenty-five thousand each?"

Lombardo nodded absently. "I guess she did," he said, "at least for a while. But this is where it gets good. She was hired by Tom Webb just before the election as a fund-raiser, like we have in the file. What you're not going to believe is that she was skimming. This was how she was going to make all that extra money. In fact, Webb, Matchett, and Cheryl were all in on it, according to Varley. The three of them were embezzling from the campaign fund, reporting only about two thirds and keeping the rest."

Gilbert felt the enervating tug of gravity pulling him into his chair. You could never entirely control a murder investigation. If it led you into a cesspool of political corruption, you had to jump right in.

"Did he know anything about Scuba-Tex?" asked Gilbert.

"No."

"Can we believe Varley?"

"Matchett threatened him," said Lombardo. "He threatened Donna as well."

"Threatened them with what?" asked Gilbert.

"He gave them an ultimatum. He offered them three thousand dollars each. If they bothered Cheryl after that, he would kill them. They asked for five thousand each, but Matchett stayed firm at three thousand, and pulled his gun to prove the point. Larry had no interest in bothering Cheryl after that. He took his three thousand dollars and invested it in his cigarette smuggling scheme. He would have made a killing, too, if we hadn't put an APB out on his vehicle." Lombardo took a deep breath and shrugged. "Then there's Donna. I guess she got greedy, or maybe she needed the money for her cocaine habit, but after the three thousand, she asked again, even though Larry told her not to. A week later she was murdered. No definite proof Matchett was her killer, but Varley's convinced of it."

In the silence that ensued, both men stared at Gilbert's desk.

"What do we do about the embezzlement?" Lombardo finally asked.

Gilbert threw up his hands in a feckless gesture of exhaustion. "We make Webb pay," he said. "We call the OPP, the financial crimes section."

"Isn't that Matchett's old section?"

Gilbert frowned; he had forgotten this. "Ah, shit. It's going to happen to Alvin all over again. His own people are going to crucify him."

The rain beat against the window. "I'm sorry, Barry."

Gilbert contemplated Lombardo. "He was a good cop," he said.

"I don't doubt it."

"But the Dennison shooting ruined him."

They again lapsed into silence. Then Lombardo spoke up.

"Did Brett get back to you today?" he asked.

Gilbert nodded, looked under some papers on his desk, and pulled out the Cabbagetown Animal Clinic case file. "Here it is," he said. "Two thousand doses. The place is right around the corner from Matchett's."

The two detectives were just getting ready to leave for the night when Carol Reid came down the aisle, her face stony, her eyes cold, and dropped the evening edition of the *Toronto Star* on Gilbert's desk.

Front-page news, story by Ronald Roffey, with a half-inch headline: WEBB'S SECRETARY ARRESTED IN LATHAM SLAYING.

And below, a large color photo of Bill Marsh escorting a handcuffed Jane Ireland down the steps of the Parliament Buildings to a waiting unmarked car.

Chapter Seventeen

Gilbert stared at Jane Ireland through the one-way glass; and he knew just by looking at her, sitting there in the interrogation room, that she was innocent, that all the evidence against her had been orchestrated by someone, a cop, who knew everything there was to know about evidence. But Marsh wouldn't listen. Marsh stood next to him with his hands on his hips. Lombardo leaned against the wall, watching everything cautiously.

"As far as I'm concerned, it's a closed case," said Marsh. "We have enough to convict. I'm marking it black on the board. The two of you are back in rotation starting tomorrow."

"You're making a mistake, Bill."

"Anyone could have burgled that animal clinic," said Marsh, turning on him. "How do you know it was Matchett?"

Gilbert gestured toward Jane. "Has she confessed?"

Marsh's lips tightened and he looked at Jane in exasperation. "Not yet," he said, "but she will."

"Has she asked to see her lawyer?"

"She says she has nothing to hide."

"I think we should get her lawyer for her."

"You let her make that decision, Barry." Marsh looked at Gilbert in frustrated mystification. "Sometimes I wonder about you, detective. Whose side are you on anyway?"

"Right now, I'm on Jane's. All I'm asking is for you to give us a chance with her. We're the primaries on this case. We know more about it than anyone else."

"I know just as much as you," said Marsh.

"You brought her in at four," said Lombardo. "She hasn't told you a thing. Maybe it's time for a change of pace. She's not some pool-hall drug dealer, Bill. You can't browbeat her that way."

"She's going down, Lombardo. You may think otherwise, but she's going down. I don't care. Talk to her. Talk to her all you want. But after that, it's over. You're back in rotation. I don't want either of you looking at the case file until the Crown decides to indict her."

"Do us a favor," said Gilbert. "Hold off on the arraignment. Give us till Monday."

Marsh looked at him incredulously. "Are you deaf, detective? I said that's it. No more man-hours, no more resources. The thing is finished. Buried. Dead."

Marsh looked first at Gilbert, then at Lombardo, a thin ribbon of sweat etching a shiny line down the side of his face.

"And if Matchett is the one who burgled the animal clinic?" said Gilbert.

"Then it's Brett's case, isn't it?" he said. "You go in and talk to Jane all you like." Marsh looked at his watch. "But you're on your own time. And when you get here tomorrow try helping out Groves, Telford, and Halycz for a change." He took one last belligerent glance at Jane. "I'm going for supper. Tell her I'll be back in an hour."

Gilbert and Lombardo entered the interrogation room quietly. Jane wasn't angry anymore . . . she looked more amused by the whole thing. The interrogation room, first room on the left as you entered the Homicide Office, was sparsely furnished: a table, a few chairs on coasters, tube lights overhead, a video camera and microphone in the corner. Gilbert looked at her arms. Under the expensive weave of her red blazer, he saw muscle, well-defined biceps and bulging pecs above her breasts. She was immaculately made up, a woman who was in charge of her appearance, and in control of her life. She appraised Gilbert.

"Detective . . ." she said, fishing for his name.

"Gilbert," he said. "We met when I first came to see Mr. Webb." He nodded toward Lombardo. "This is my partner, Joe Lombardo."

She looked at Joe with glassy eyes and a frozen smile. "How do you do," she said.

"Fine," he said.

"Can I get you anything?" asked Gilbert. "A sandwich? Coffee?"

"I"m careful with my diet," she said. "I'll have something when I get home."

She was absolutely convinced she was going to leave headquarters tonight.

"Do you know why you're here?" he asked.

"Detective Marsh arrested me for the murder of Cheryl Latham," she said.

"And he informed you of your rights?" said Lombardo.

"Yes, he did."

"And you've decided against having a lawyer present," said Gilbert.

"For the time being."

The two detectives sat down. Gilbert leaned forward, put his elbows on the table, and rubbed his hands together. He glanced at the video camera. The situation was delicate. He didn't want to undercut Marsh's authority or convey in any way to Jane Ireland that the MTPF moved on anything but a consolidated front.

"Did Staff Inspector Marsh outline any of the evidence against you?" he asked.

"He mentioned the bullet," she said.

. She ran her hand over her forehead, frowning, as if she had a headache.

"Are you all right?" asked Gilbert. "You're sure I can't get you anything."

"No."

"You look tired."

"I'm not tired," she said. "I'm never tired. I can't afford to be tired."

Gilbert decided he was going to save a lot of time. "You were set up by Matchett, weren't you?"

She seemed to freeze. She looked at Gilbert, sat up straight, her neck extending. She reminded Gilbert of an exotic bird, a heron or flamingo looking up over the reeds, alerted to danger.

"I don't even know how to work a gun," she said. "I have no idea how that bullet got there."

"We know Matchett took you up to his club," said Gilbert.

"I went only because it was one of the few times in the week we got to go out together," she said.

"And you never fired the weapon?" said Lombardo. "Not even out of curiosity."

She turned to Lombardo. "I hate guns," she said.

"So how do you explain the bullet behind your filing cabinet?" asked Gilbert

"I can't. He knew I detested guns. I wouldn't let him bring it into the apartment."

"So where did he keep it?" said Lombardo.

"He kept it at his place."

"And what about the boots?" said Gilbert.

"You'll find an identical pair of boots at his place. Which is exactly what I told Staff Inspector Marsh."

"Why would he buy an identical pair of boots?" said Lombardo.

"I think that's obvious," said Jane.

"So you agree with us then," said Gilbert. "You think Matchett was trying to stage you."

"You stay with Alvin for a while, you get to know him, you live with him, and you begin to see that something's not right about him. I finally told him to get out last June."

"He told us he was the one who left you. That you took it hard," said Gilbert.

"You see what I mean?" She sat back in her chair and glanced first at Lombardo then at Gilbert. "I asked him to give me my key back. He said he lost it. I've been after my landlord to get the locks changed since June. Alvin said he lost it but I know he didn't. I'd come home and I'd find small things missing. Stupid things. Soap. Ketchup. My hairbrush. He thought I didn't know." She shook her head. "But I knew. I called the police but they said there was nothing they could do, that unless they caught him red-handed—"

"He took your hairbrush?" asked Gilbert.

She nodded.

"Because we found three strands of your hair on Cheryl's body."

She again grew still. She leaned forward and rubbed her

hands together. Then her shoulders sank. "I guess you just answered your own question, detective. And as for taking it hard, I was overjoyed when it ended. I felt like I got my life back. You always get the sense with Alvin that he's somehow positioning himself for advantage. Oh, he can be charming, but underneath that charm he cares for no one but himself."

Gilbert felt Joe watching him; this was hard, listening to his old partner described this way. "So you think he planted the hair," said Gilbert.

"I liked Cheryl," she said. "Things were going on, I don't know what. Funny things. Especially around election time. I was concerned about her. She got involved with Alvin and I knew it couldn't be good. I saw a lot of unexplained cancelled checks. Sometimes the two of them stayed late at night. Often Tom was there with them. Alvin was acting really strange. He kept watching me. I knew something was up. The money kept going to the same place, just a number, a corporation, but there were never any particulars, no description of the services rendered. Campaign support, that's all it ever said. And Alvin kept watching me. He wasn't subtle. Obviously they were trying to hide something. Any fool could see that. And I wasn't any fool. So all this—this hair, the boots, the bullet—it all makes sense. I can't say why he killed Cheryl, if in fact he did. Pinning all this on me makes me think he did. The poor girl. Near the end, he was watching her the same way he was watching me. Like he was just waiting. And Cheryl was so nervous. I think she was glad when the election was finally over."

Gilbert and Lombardo looked at each other. "So there's no love wasted between you and Alvin?" said Gilbert.

"You're kidding," she said, dryly.

"He gave me the impression he still loved you."

"He's manipulating you, just like he manipulates everybody. Just like he manipulated Cheryl."

"What was Cheryl like during the election?"

Jane paused to think. "She was like . . ." She gazed at the video camera. "She was like a small girl who had been asked to pilot a jumbo jet through a narrow mountain passage. Only she didn't know the first thing about planes. Webb asked me a few questions once. I knew he was sounding me out. I hate to say this, but I think Tom . . . he's a wonderful man, an asset to the party, and he . . . but I really think—"

"What about the car?"

She nodded. "That was Marsh's trump card."

Gilbert nodded. "Marsh is a good detective," he said, conscious of the video camera.

"A message was left on my machine while I was on afternoon coffee," she said. "I was to leave a car in the Mount Joseph parking lot."

"Who left the message?"

"Tom did."

Gilbert had to take a few seconds for this to sink in. Was Webb going to turn out to be an accomplice in his stepdaughter's murder?

"Why the Mount Joseph parking lot?" he asked.

A few lines came to Jane's brow. "That's the strange part," she said. "I looked in his engagement book and he wasn't scheduled for Mount Joseph that night. His schedule was open. I couldn't figure out what he would be doing down at Mount Joseph anyway. I thought it might have something to do with Dorothy."

"Dorothy?"

"His wife," she said. "Cheryl's mother. She died there three years ago. I was constantly bringing cars down to the Mount Joseph parking lot for him. He stayed late, often until the small hours of the morning."

"What did he say?" asked Gilbert.

"Who, Tom?"

"Did you mention it to him the next morning?"

"We had an argument about it. An hour or so before you got there."

"What did he say?"

"He said he never asked for a car."

"Did you play him the tape?"

"I'd erased the tape by that time. I do it every evening before I go."

"But you're sure it was his voice."

"Positive. I've worked for the man for the last ten years."

"And he denied it?" said Lombardo.

"He denied it."

"And you erased the tape and now it's your word against his," said Gilbert. "Maybe Tom was getting nervous about you too. This money thing, we're digging into it, and it doesn't look good. He was nervous about you so he arranged for you to get the car."

She shook her head. "It still doesn't make sense," she said. "Why Mount Joseph? And why would he leave his own voice on my voice mail when he knew perfectly well he would be incriminated by it?"

"Did anyone see you drop the car?"

"No. They have an automated attendant now."

"Did you leave it any particular place?" asked Gilbert.

"Up on level 3, near the back."

Gilbert looked at Lombardo. "I'll check it out," said the younger detective.

"But you're right," said Gilbert. "Why Mount Joseph? Why not closer to Cheryl's place? Why a spot where any number of hospital employees might see it? There's a gap here. And I don't know what it is."

They left College Street just after nine that evening and went for a drink at the Duke of York, an English pub on

Prince Arthur not far from Varsity Arena. A place of heavy green Victorian-style wallpaper and dark mahogany furniture, the Duke served primarily imported beer from England, Newcastle Brown Ale, Guinness, Double Diamond, and was frequented mainly by Toronto's small but close-knit English and Scottish communities. Both detectives liked the place because of its cozy atmosphere and lack of pretense. They went to the downstairs pub and found a table at the back. Gilbert made a quick call to Regina, then ordered a pint of Toby.

The two detectives watched the pub crowd for a while. Gilbert tried not to brood, but he couldn't help it. He tried to put it in perspective, how such a good cop could do something so bad, but the change seemed too great. He had to fight to reconcile the discrepancy and was barely able to make the crossover. The waitresses here were young, pretty, British, and bosomy. Joe seemed entirely distracted by them. But then his young partner said,

"So what are we going to do?"

He contemplated Lombardo as if from a long distance. His memories kept getting in the way of everything tonight. He and Matchett, in uniform, in the radio car, the best cops 52 Division ever saw. How could Matchett have turned inside out like that?

"Are you being rhetorical?" said Gilbert.

Lombardo looked away, put off. Gilbert didn't mean to be cruel to Joe, he just felt rotten tonight. Lombardo sensed this.

"I'm sorry about Matchett," said Lombardo.

Gilbert stared at the foam in his beer. "The moment I found the bank statements in the birdcage I knew it had to be him," he said. "He's terrified of birds. She must have let the bird out of the cage the night he came to get her. She tried to spook him. He caught the bird and killed it. If you had to hide documents from a man who was terrified of birds, where would you hide them?"

"He should have checked the cage," said Lombardo. "The bird was dead."

"Aversions work in strange ways," said Gilbert. "They create blind spots. The birdcage was a blind spot for Alvin."

Lombardo shrugged. "Maybe," he said. "I'm just sorry it had to be . . . we might be wrong. Maybe Jane's the one."

"She's agreed to a polygraph," said Gilbert. "If she's lying, she wouldn't have gone for the polygraph. And it's not only that." He took a sip of beer, but he couldn't enjoy it. "The whole manner of the crime points to Alvin. The care he took with the search. The lack of fingerprints. Even the bullet to her chest."

"What do you mean?"

"She was already dead," said Gilbert. "Blackstein has cause of death as hypothermia. Why shoot her? I'll tell you why. Because Alvin shot Laraby three times at close range, we thought the guy was dead, but he turned out to be alive, and he grabbed my revolver from my holster and shot me twice. So Alvin emptied another four rounds into him. The guy wouldn't die. That's why he was thorough with Dennison, and that's why he was thorough with Cheryl. He could have dumped her without the overkill, but Laraby was still in the back of his mind and he wasn't going to take any chances. Over and above all that, we have Larry Varley's story. We have to face facts, Joe. Alvin did it. I hate it, it really leaves me sour, it takes the glow away from my patrol days, I hate what I'm going to have to do to him, but that's my job, and I'm going to nail him."

"Which brings us back to my first question," said Lombardo. "What are we going to do?"

"We're going to nail him."

"What about Webb? What about the message Jane got about the car?"

"We leave it. Alvin will be that much more likely to bolt if we start asking Webb questions. We'll worry about Webb later."

"So we're going to nail Matchett," said Lombardo. "How exactly are we going to do that? As far as Marsh is concerned, the case is closed. No more man-hours, no more resources. We're back in rotation tomorrow."

"No," said Gilbert, "we're not. Between the Kedamine and the gun, we've easily got enough for a search warrant. First thing in the morning I go to the Park."

"Alvin'll run if we search his place. He has a quarter million dollars waiting for him in the Bahamas."

"We'll search it when he's not there."

"He'll still know. He's a cop. He'll leave a hair on the top of the door. He'll use any one of those old tricks. He'll come back, he'll see we've been there. Maybe we should go straight for the arrest warrant."

"I don't think we have enough for the arrest warrant yet. We've got to at least connect him to the Cabbagetown Animal Clinic. Then we can hold him on both a burglary and a drug charge. But first we've got to find Kedamine in his apartment."

"Yeah, but what do we do between the time of the search and the time of the arrest? Tell him not to go anywhere? He'll run for sure."

Gilbert gazed at the foam on the top of his beer. "I guess it's stakeout time, then," he said.

Lombardo's eyes widened. "Are you crazy? After the search, you'll be writing the arrest warrant and I'll be twisting arms at the lab to get priority for whatever we find. Who's going to watch him? You think Marsh won't be checking our every move?"

"Halycz and Groves will look after Marsh," said Gilbert. "We'll put Telford on Alvin. Gord's always been good at that kind of thing."

Lombardo glanced at one of the big-bosomed waitresses, but he seemed to derive no enjoyment from it. "So all five of us are going to take a fall over this."

"I'm detective-sergeant, aren't I?"

"I know, but I—"

"Don't worry, Joe." Gilbert now nearly felt happy about all the resistance he faced. "The only one who's going to take a fall over this is Marsh."

Jane Ireland cooperated fully, even though she was resentful about her continued detainment; she gave Gilbert and Lombardo her copy of the key to Matchett's apartment.

At ten o'clock Friday morning, March 6, the snow had stopped and the skies were clearing and all the slush was starting to freeze. Gilbert and Lombardo were parked down the street, on the corner of Sackville and Winchester. The radio cackled. Telford sent a message via dispatch that the suspect had just entered his place of work, the Parliament Buildings.

Gilbert and Lombardo got out of the car and walked to Matchett's.

They climbed the stairs to the third floor.

As they opened the door, a small piece of paper toppled out from between the jamb and the latch. The two detectives looked at each other. Then they proceeded with their search. They did the search themselves. They had to. They were working behind Marsh's back.

Gilbert checked the medicine cabinet; he swept the entire contents into an evidence bag, even though there was nothing in there that looked like Kedamine.

"Hey, look at this," called Lombardo from the other room. "He's got another gun."

Gilbert came out of the bathroom to the dining room. An old Smith and Wesson .38 caliber revolver sat on the table in an open briefcase next to some cleaning equipment and ammunition.

"Should we take it?" said Lombardo.

Gilbert shook his head. "No," he said. "It's not in the warrant. I'd hate to bugger things up on a technicality. But if you find the Heckler and Koch, it's ours. I've got it listed."

They searched until nearly eleven. The Kedamine was nowhere to be found. Neither was the Heckler and Koch. They found some tools—a crowbar, a hammer, a screwdriver—implements that might have been used in the burglary, and which, when tested, might show a chemical match to the animal clinic's exterior paint or other construction materials. But they both realized they were grasping now. Gilbert stood in the hall while Lombardo went through the kitchen one last time. He stared. Thinking. Wondering what else they could do. He stared, but stared without looking. But then he began to look. And he was looking at the partially open hall closet, something they had already checked through twice. Nothing but coats in there. Pockets already checked. Nothing incriminating. But then he realized that he recognized one of the coats. A parka with a deep hood.

"Joe," he said, "look at this."

Lombardo came out of the kitchen and looked at the coat. And his eyes narrowed. He glanced at Gilbert. "Isn't that from . . ."

"It's from the Glenarden video."

He stared at the coat as his mind ran through the possibilities. Not only had they placed Matchett at the Glenarden on the night of the eighteenth, but chemical analysis of the pocket linings might reveal trace amounts of Kedamine.

He looked more closely. Grease stains. From where? Maybe from the laundry room window.

"We've got him," he said.

*   *   *

By noon they were back at College Street with the vouchered evidence. They radioed Telford to let him know. By twelve-thirty the evidence was in the lab. Because the technicians knew they were looking for Kedamine, Gilbert and Lombardo thought they might get an identification soon. Meanwhile Gilbert worked frantically on the arrest warrant, including the drug and burglary angle, risking the murder aspect on a separate sheet. Telford car-phoned him a little after one.

"He's leaving the Parliament Buildings," he said.

And later: "He's getting into his car and driving east on Wellesley."

And still later. "He's turned left on Winchester," said Telford. "He's going home."

Marsh stared at Gilbert suspiciously from across the room. "Stick with him," said Gilbert. "Don't let him out of your sight. The minute I have this thing signed I want you to go in and arrest him."

For the next half hour Marsh hovered nearby and Gilbert was forced to work on a new case, a murder-suicide out in Scarborough. But Marsh finally tired, and walked in the direction of the atrium. Gilbert continued working on his warrant.

Shortly before two, Lombardo came back from the lab. "It's going to be a while," he said. "I thought I'd run down to Gord Danby's office and play him the tape. Do you got it?"

Gilbert opened the drawer of his desk and pulled out a mini-cassette. Lunch at the Raj-Shala, Alvin's voice, something they hoped Gord Danby would recognize from the bogus travel agent call. Lombardo took the tape and slid it in his pocket.

"The lab has your number," said Lombardo. "They're going to call you as soon they have anything. Everything's under a new file name now, in case Marsh tries to call the lab."

Lombardo wrote down the file name and gave it to Gilbert.

"He's going to bolt," said Gilbert. "Telford's there right now. He's going to bolt no matter how fast we get this down. He's making plans right now. His parka's gone, his tools are gone, everything in his medicine cabinet is gone. If it weren't for Marsh, I'd have the place surrounded with radio cars right now. But we haven't even got an outstanding warrant on Alvin. There's nothing we can do to stop him."

"The minute Lembeck signs that," said Lombardo, "we go. I think Telford should have backup. I'm going to take my gun. You should too. We know Matchett has at least the one weapon."

Gilbert finished the arrest warrant a half hour later. All he had to do was wait for the lab so he could fill in the details.

Just before three the lab called him. Trace amounts of Kedamine had been found in the pocket linings of Matchett's parka. Microscopic paint samples from the crowbar matched the samples taken from the receiving door at the Cabbagetown Animal Clinic. As far as Gilbert was concerned that was enough for the duty judge at College Park.

He was just putting on his coat and hat when Lombardo called.

"Gord Danby positively identified Matchett's voice," said Joe.

Gilbert filled in the last detail on the arrest warrant and hurried across the street. But not without first grabbing his gun.

When Gilbert explained the pressing nature of the situation to Judge Lembeck, the judge scribbled his signature along the bottom of the document without hesitation.

"Thanks, Dave," said Gilbert.

"I'll risk a burglary and narcotics for you, Barry," said the judge. "I'm holding off on this murder thing for now. You still have enough to hold him. But for Christ's sake, Barry, be careful. This guy sounds dangerous."

Chapter Eighteen

Lombardo picked up Gilbert in front of College Park just as the afternoon rush hour began to thicken.

"I was just talking to Telford," said Gilbert. "Alvin's still there. He didn't return to work after lunch. I don't like this."

Lombardo pulled out into traffic and eased across Yonge Street. Maple Leaf Gardens loomed to the left.

"I thought you said the only way in and out of his place was through the front door," said Lombardo.

"Forget what I said," replied Gilbert. "We're dealing with Alvin. And Alvin is good."

They turned north on Parliament and drove to Winchester. They found Telford waiting in his unmarked car a half block down. All three detectives got out of their respective cars and conferred by the curb.

"It's been quiet," said Telford, a red-faced man of about forty. "No one's come in or out. I've seen no movement in the windows. He pulled that blind down on the third floor shortly after he got home."

Gilbert stared up at the old Edwardian house, a squat red brick dwelling with a steep slate roof and ornate trim around each dormer, a typical middle-class dwelling of ninety years ago now divided into three modern renovated apartments. Matchett's white Ford Tempo was parked out front. Gilbert took a deep breath as a garbage truck rumbled by. The wind was building and he could feel his nose turning red.

"All right," he said at last. "Do you have your gun, Gord?" he asked Telford.

"I've got a shotgun in the trunk."

"You might as well get it," said Gilbert. "Try not to shoot unless you absolutely have to. We know he has a revolver. That doesn't mean he won't have something else."

Telford went around to the trunk and pulled out a Remington Model 870 shotgun, and checked the seven-round magazine to make sure it was full. The three detectives walked across the street. Telford concealed, as best he could, the shotgun under his coat. Gilbert took out the key Jane Ireland had given him. They climbed the steps and pushed their way into the vestibule. And Gilbert immediately knew Matchett was gone. The door to the first-floor apartment had been broken open. But he pulled out his gun just in case. The other detectives did the same.

He gazed down the hall of the first-floor apartment. He saw a kitchen at the back, and sliding glass doors leading out to a deck. A Persian cat peeked around the living room door, stared at them, then licked its pug nose a few times.

"Shit," he said. "Joe, you go in there and check it out. Gord and I will go upstairs."

Lombardo, keeping his gun aimed at the ceiling, his elbow sharply bent, proceeded into the first-floor apartment. Gilbert and Telford climbed the stairs. He hated enclosed stairwells like this; there was nowhere to hide. They climbed slowly, weapons ready, placing each footstep carefully to minimize noise. Up to the second-floor landing, past the umbrella stand the second-floor tenant had outside the door, pausing at the foot of the third-floor stairs and listening. Nothing from upstairs. He looked back at Telford and nodded. The two detectives climbed the third-floor stairs and stopped outside Matchett's door. Silence. Gilbert put his ear to the door, then slid the key into the lock, turned it, and pushed the door open in one quick motion.

He swung toward the kitchen and the bedroom, gun clasped in both hands, arms outstretched, while Telford turned left, covering the living room. Gilbert quickly proceeded into the kitchen, where evidence of a quick lunch—a half-finished bagel and an apple with a bite out of it—sat on the table. He moved down the hall past the bathroom and finally into the bedroom. Dresser drawers were open. A half full suitcase sat on the unmade bed. The closet was open and some shirts were on the floor.

"Clear!" called Telford.

Gilbert checked the bedside table drawer. The Smith and Wesson was gone, and in and among some gun magazines he saw some loose ammunition.

"Clear," he called.

Telford appeared at the bedroom door, walked around the bed, and over to the window.

"Look at this," he said.

Gilbert glanced out the window. He saw a backyard. There was a gate leading to an alley. The alley led all the way up to Wellesley Street. Gilbert shook his head to himself.

"Marsh pisses me off," he said.

Telford shrugged. "There's a bunch of hair on the floor in the bathroom."

The two men left the bedroom and checked the bathroom. Not only was there hair on the floor, but there was a bit in the toilet and some in the sink. Alvin was good. He was going to use all the fugitive tricks.

"Everything clear?" Lombardo called from down the stairs.

"Yeah, we're clear," called Gilbert.

A moment later, Lombardo appeared at the bathroom door. He slid his .38 into his shoulder holster.

"He gave himself a make-over?" he asked.

Gilbert nodded. "He figured things out," he said. "He knows how we're moving."

"Where would he go?" asked Telford.

"He's got a quarter million dollars stashed in the Bahamas," said Lombardo.

"He's probably halfway to the airport by now," said Gilbert. "If this were SOP I'd be calling all cars. But we've got Marsh standing in our way." Gilbert left the bathroom and marched to the kitchen phone, his trench coat flapping with sudden speed. The other detectives followed. "So we have to do this one ourselves." He lifted the receiver. "I wonder if Alvin knows this one? You see this handset? It's got a redial button. It automatically redials the last number called. I wonder if he was smart enough to decoy an anonymous number into the phone before he left." Gilbert pressed the redial button and put the receiver to his ear. "Maybe he left us a whopping big clue."

Matchett, as it turned out, hadn't left a decoy number on the handset. "Canadian Airlines," a pleasant female voice said.

"Yes, when is your next flight to Freeport, the Bahamas?" asked Gilbert.

"We have two seats left on our six o'clock flight," said the woman, "and five on our eleven-thirty flight."

"Do you have the name Matchett on the flight manifest for the six o'clock flight?" asked Gilbert.

"One moment, sir," said the woman. Gilbert heard the faint clicking of computer keys. "Yes, sir. A Mr. Matchett is on that flight. Is there a message for him, sir?"

Gilbert looked at his watch. Just past four. An hour out to the airport, an hour-and-a-half in rush hour. They might be able to shave time if they put the light on the roof.

"No," said Gilbert. "No message."

The three detectives got in Gilbert's unmarked car.

They sped north on Parliament Street and veered right at Bloor Street past the St. James Cemetery, over the Prince Edward Viaduct. They continued east over the Bloor-Danforth Viaduct and spiraled down the steep on-ramp to the Don Valley Parkway. They headed north through the Valley, unable to move much faster than the marked speed limit of 90 kph through the thickening rush-hour traffic. At the single lane westbound feeder to the 401, traffic bottlenecked and they had to slow right down. But once they got onto the 401, with its six lanes of westbound traffic, Gilbert slalomed through the slower moving cars and deftly maneuvered into the express lanes. It was just past five when they passed the Allen Expressway.

"They'll probably board a half hour in advance," said Gilbert. "If we have to, we'll take him in the plane."

They roared under the Allen Expressway cloverleaf, where the 401 snaked around overpass pillars, the tires squealing as they took the banked curves in excess of 140 kph. Then traffic thickened again, and Gilbert was forced to ease up on the accelerator as the collector lanes ended and the highway narrowed from twelve to six lanes. After such high speeds, Gilbert felt as if they were crawling. They moved through a wasteland of suburban hotels and light industrial parkland. The sun was going down and hung like a big orange ball, shining through the chemical haze on the horizon. Square green airport signs dotted the highway every kilometer or so. They were getting close, but they still had to find the right gate, and then the right boarding lounge. And then they had to identify Matchett. Who knows what he had done to his appearance?

Jets swept low over the highway now, their nighttime landing lights piercing the encroaching gloom like laser shafts.

"We're not going to make it if we go south on 427," said Gilbert. "I think it might be better if we take the 409."

"But that takes you to Terminal 3," said Lombardo. "We want Terminal 1."

Tightly packed red taillights moved bumper to bumper about a mile ahead.

"Look at that," said Gilbert. "That's stop and go. And the 409's just up here. And there's never anybody on the 409."

But even the exit ramp to the 409 was still a considerable distance, and it was quarter past five now.

Gilbert gave Lombardo a gruff nod. "Put the light on the roof," he said. "I'm going on the shoulder."

Lombardo took the red light from under the dash, opened the window, and stuck it on the roof. A fitful scarlet flicker lit the surrounding cars and trucks. A DC 7 screeched low overhead. Gilbert swerved to the shoulder and stepped on the gas. The guardrail felt uncomfortably close, but that couldn't be helped. They reached the exit ramp to the 409 in less than a minute.

Gilbert now had two lanes of traffic to himself. The unmarked Lumina, light still flashing, climbed to 160 kph; even over the most minute hump in the road the car felt as if it took flight. Up ahead he now saw the control tower. Jets were taking off and landing in every direction. He saw the Airport Hilton, the Sheridan, the Days Inn, the Holiday Inn, and the Four Seasons glittering on the horizon, modern buildings that caught and reflected the blood-red sky to the west. He eased on the brake as the Airport Road exit loomed ahead of them. He swerved to the right, taking the 50-kph ramp at 90 kph, ran the red light at the turnoff, and bolted left toward Terminal 1. They passed a barrage of signs—Departures, Arrivals, Parking, Customs—and finally swung into the giant covered portico of Terminal 1.

Gilbert looked in the rearview mirror at Telford. "You're not going to look too great carrying that shotgun around inside." Lombardo killed the light and clipped it under the dash. "You stay here in case he makes a try for it out this way." He looked at Lombardo. "You ready?"

Lombardo's face was hard. "Let's do it."

The partners got out of the car and marched in through the revolving doors.

Terminal 1 was a long corridor-like structure punctuated by plastic-chaired waiting areas, duty-free shops, and a multitude of various airline kiosks.

"Gate Five, wasn't it?" said Gilbert.

"That's way at the other end," said Lombardo.

"Shit," said Gilbert. "He'll be in pre-boarding by now, if not already on the jet."

The detectives began running, attracting the stares of the heavier-than-usual Friday night throng of international travellers.

At Gate Five, three dozen sun-seekers bound for the Bahamas crowded the entrance to the boarding lounge as a travel agent wearing a bright yellow blazer handed out complimentary travel bags. The detectives pushed their way through the crowd. Some of the sun-seekers grumbled. Gilbert flashed them his shield.

At the front of the line, behind the barrier at a high counter, a prim young Canadian Airlines representative said, "Sir, I'm sorry, but it's passengers only beyond this point."

He showed the young woman his badge. "Metro Homicide," he said. "We have reason to believe a fugitive may be trying to board this plane. Please keep these passengers clear of the boarding area until we make sure everything's safe."

The woman gave him a stunned little nod. A murmuring swept thought the crowd of sun-seekers. Gilbert and Lombardo pushed through.

They followed a long corridor that angled periodically in segments out toward the runway area. At the end of the corridor they came to the pre-boarding lounge for Flight 237 to Freeport. Out the large windows they saw the nose of a Canadian Airlines 737 pressing close to the glass. An enclosed rampway right-angled toward the forward cabin door. Passengers were lined up at the beginning of the rampway, about thirty in all, some already in shorts, T-shirts, and sun hats. Gilbert scanned the crowd but he couldn't see Matchett anywhere. A flight attendant came out and helped a man in a wheelchair through the barrier.

"They're doing pre-boarding," said Gilbert.

"Do you see him?"

Gilbert shook his head. "He's going to wait until the last minute. He knows we can nail him easier here. This was just a long shot. He's still out in the terminal. He knows he has to get rid of his gun before he passes the security checkpoint. He's going to hang onto it as long as he can before he boards."

"We can wait here for him," said Lombardo. "Over there, behind those vending machines."

Gilbert shook his head again. "Too risky," he said. "He'll be looking for us here." Outside they heard the rise and fall of the 737's jet engines as the turbines began to gear up for the flight. "I think we stand a better chance if we try and surprise him out in the terminal."

Lombardo nodded. "Then's let do it."

They ran down the long corridor out past the barrier. Gilbert cleared things with the Canadian Airlines representative.

"Try and detain any last-minute passengers as long as you can," he said.

They hurried out to the terminal.

Gilbert took one side of the terminal and Lombardo took the other, making a slow westward sweep of the modern glass and steel structure, maintaining eye contact with each other. They moved past all the airline kiosks and duty-free shops, the newsstands and drug stores, scanning the crowds, looking for a tall, slim toughly built man who had altered his hair in some way. A woman's voice over the PA announced that Flight 237 was now boarding for Freeport, would passengers please proceed to Gate Five. And it dawned on Gilbert yet again just how much was at stake: if Matchett got away, it would mean Joe's job, maybe his own, and most probably prison time for Jane Ireland. Worst of all, there would be no justice for Cheryl Latham and Donna Varley.

A baggage handler pushed a huge cart of luggage in front of him.

And when the cart moved out of the way . . . Gilbert stopped . . . and stared . . .

Stopped because he saw a tall man, completely bald, with a pair of sunglasses astride his nose. The tall man stood inside Lichtman's Books, near the back, reading a gun magazine, his face nearly buried in the pages. Gilbert peered more closely at the man; he recognized the cleft chin, the tawny eyebrows, the prominent but narrow nose. Gilbert lifted his hand, signaling to Lombardo . . . and just as Gilbert lifted his hand for Lombardo, Matchett looked up. And saw Gilbert.

His old partner from patrol looked at him through his sunglasses. Gilbert saw regret, bitterness, exhaustion, sadness, but most of all, determination. Matchett dropped the magazine, and, abandoning his luggage on the floor of Lichtman's, bolted from the bookstore and ran westward through the terminal. Gilbert and Lombardo ran after him. Matchett dodged in and around stunned travellers, knocking a couple of teenagers to the floor. He pulled his gun and fired a shot toward the ceiling. Everyone panicked, dove, ran, jumped for cover, creating a multitude of obstacles for Gilbert and Lombardo. Gilbert had to shove several people out of the way. He stumbled into an elderly man, knocking him down, but kept going, never losing sight of Matchett. He glanced to the other side of the terminal. Lombardo high-jumped over a prostrate young couple; at thirty-two, Lombardo had the better pair of lungs. Gilbert did his best, but in seconds Lombardo was way ahead of him. And he didn't like that because he didn't want Joe to face Matchett one-on-one, especially when Matchett practiced so vigorously at the range once a week. So he turned on as much juice as he could, pushing his forty-eight-year-old heart to the limit, glad he had at least kept up with his swimming.

Matchett took an aborted turn at the terminal's center doors, but he must have seen their unmarked car, so kept running. Lombardo ran diagonally from his side of the terminal, taking two rows of chairs like an Olympic hurdler, veering back on course when he got to Gilbert's side of the terminal. Gilbert had never seen Lombardo run like that before; his legs and arms were a blur; he was quickly gaining on Matchett. A mother pulled her small children to the floor as Lombardo ran by. Gilbert drew his gun. He dreaded the prospect, but he might actually have to shoot Matchett.

Matchett finally ducked out the far doors of Terminal 1. A moment later Lombardo did the same. Gilbert was breathing hard, wanted to stop, but kept a steady pace.

Fifteen seconds later, he himself exited out the far doors.

The sky was dark now. Down a hill past the terminal's

drive-through was an outdoor parking lot. Beyond this there loomed a multi-level indoor parking lot. In the glare of the overhead lights it was hard to see. He ran across the drive-through and stood at the top of the hill. He saw tracks in the snow. He thought he should get Telford but then decided there just wasn't time. About a hundred-and-fifty cars were parked in the lot below.

And now he heard gunfire. And saw a figure, crouched over, running, trying to hide between the parked cars. He heard answering gunfire, and a windshield shattered. Now he saw Joe, crouched low over the trunk of a BMW, arms extended, taking aim. *Blam!* A muzzle flash brightened the trunk of the BMW. He could hardly believe this. His old partner and his new partner were firing at each other.

"Alvin!" he called. "Please . . . we'll work something out. We'll see about a plea."

But he got no answer. Lombardo ran crouched over to the next row of parked cars. Gilbert descended the slope to the parking lot, his shoes slipping on the snow. He had just reached the Pontiac at the foot of the slope when he saw Matchett dart out from behind a Ford Windstar and dash toward the multi-level parking garage. Lombardo stood, arms extended, clutching his weapon in both hands, but couldn't get a clear shot because Matchett kept crouching, moving from car to car, keeping himself well covered. Matchett climbed a small incline, pushed through some ornamental cedars, and jumped over the railing onto the first level of the multi-level parking garage. Lombardo bolted through the cars after him. In five seconds, Gilbert's young partner was up and over the barrier, chasing Matchett down the ramp that led to the underground sub-levels.

Puffing hard now, Gilbert ran across the parking lot and pulled himself over the railing. He hated multi-level parking garages; in a multi-level parking garage there were simply too many places to hide. Over the whine of an incoming jet he heard retreating footsteps from the switchback down-ramp. As he reached sub-level one, he again heard gunfire. He lifted his revolver and descended the ramp with caution, trying to get his breathing under control. He saw a series of Air Canada luggage vans parked all in a row. And at the end, lit by the pale glow of the fluorescent lights, he saw Lombardo crumpled on the concrete, as still as Cheryl, as still Donna, as still as poor Paul Varley all those many years ago, arm extended at an unnatural angle, clutching his revolver, trench coat thrown open, a pool of blood that looked purple in the fluorescent light spreading in a huge delta from the top of his head.

Gilbert felt his legs suddenly weaken. He gripped the ramp railing for support, stopping for a moment, knowing that none of this was worth Joe's life. But then he grew angry, and with anger, his training returned, and he lifted his gun, and moved slowly toward Lombardo.

"Stop where you are, Barry."

Gilbert stopped. He couldn't see Matchett but his voice had come from behind one of the Air Canada vans up to the left.

"Throw your weapon aside," said Matchett. "I don't want to do to you what I did to Joe."

"Alvin, you'll never get away," said Gilbert. "You think I haven't phoned the authorities in Freeport? Give it up. You've killed a police officer. There's no way you can get away now."

"I said throw the weapon aside, Barry. Under that Cadillac." Matchett's voice intensified. "Go on, do it! I've got fifteen minutes to make my flight."

Gilbert realized he had no choice; there was something wild in Matchett's voice.

He bent slowly at the knees, put his revolver on the concrete, and slid it the five meters to the Cadillac. He stood up.

Matchett emerged from the fifth van up on the left. And he had a smile on his face, a smile unlike any smile Gilbert had ever seen on Matchett's face. Joe remained motionless three cars back, another homicide, another red mark on the clearance board.

"Get on your knees, Barry," he said. "I want you to beg me for your life. I want you to prove to me that you're not like all those others, Ling and Marsh, and all the rest of them."

Gilbert stared at his old partner. "Alvin, I . . ."

With his bald head and sunglasses, he didn't look at all like Matchett anymore, or like a cop. He looked more like hired muscle, a hit man.

"You heard me, on your knees, detective!"

Gilbert hesitated, then finally got to his knees. Matchett walked toward him, keeping the Smith and Wesson trained on his forehead, his black cowboy boots making muffled clicks against the concrete.

"Alvin, you don't want to do this."

"What do they say these days? Payback time. That's a popular phrase these days. Only I've been thinking about it ever since I got kicked off the force. It's nothing new to me."

"Alvin, please, we can work . . . we can work something out. We'll talk to the Crown."

"The Crown can fuck itself. I'm through with the Crown." The ugly smile came back to his face. "I'm going to retire. And no one's going to stop me. Not you. Not Cheryl." He flicked his head toward Lombardo. "Certainly not Joe. I'm going to make my plane. And I can't have you running after me, trying anything . . . I know you were always one for trying things. Always a smart guy. I'm sorry, Barry. I'm really sorry. But maybe it'll leave them something to think about. Maybe they might change a few of the regulations, a few guidelines, so an officer isn't crucified every time he discharges his weapon. Maybe, in the long run, by killing you I might save the lives of a hundred officers after you."

"You can't be serious, Alvin," he said. "This is crazy."

The smile dropped from Matchett's face and the bitterness thickened in his eyes. He raised the gun, easily steady in his right hand, an old double-action model, needing a cock of the hammer before it would fire. Matchett was just pressing his thumb to the hammer when Gilbert sensed movement behind him. Lombardo raised his arm and pointed it at Matchett's back. It seemed Matchett hadn't learned his lesson from Laraby after all. The dead could still walk.

"Freeze, Matchett!" shouted Joe.

In Matchett's brief moment of surprise, Gilbert snatched the gun in a lightning sideways swipe, and launched himself head first at Matchett's solar plexus. His old partner doubled over, the wind knocked out of him. Gilbert maneuvered his thumb behind the trigger; the only way the revolver would fire now was if Matchett fanned the hammer. Lombardo got up, slipping a bit in his own blood, and staggered. He stood over Matchett, raised his .38 high in both hands, and brought the grip crashing down on top of Matchett's head.

"That's for ruining my new suit," he said, his voice breathless with rage.

Matchett slumped to one side. Lombardo yanked him from Gilbert and kneed him in the back.

"That's for wrecking my new haircut," he said.

He forced the now stunned Matchett face down on the concrete, wrenched his arms behind his back, and cuffed him. The metallic click of the handcuffs had a finality about it.

"And that's for what you did to Cheryl and Donna."

Then all the energy seemed to go out of Lombardo. He sat down, like a child in a sandbox, legs out but knees partially bent, toes pointing skyward. His face was messy with blood. He looked at Gilbert, as if he just realized for the first time that Gilbert was next to him.

"You okay?" asked the young detective.

Gilbert got into a squatting position next to Joe and had a quick look at his head wound. "I'm fine," he said. The wound was a graze, nothing serious, but enough to knock Lombardo unconscious for a few minutes. "What about you?"

Lombardo nodded, swallowed. "Fine," he said. He looked at Matchett and gave the prostrate man a last final kick with the heel of his foot. "Never felt better."

Chapter Nineteen

On Monday morning, after getting his coffee and muffin upstairs, Gilbert took the elevator back down to Homicide. The lights were off in Marsh's office. Usually he was here before everybody else. Now all Gilbert saw were the dark silhouettes of Marsh's office furniture and a dull grey sky beyond. He wove his way through the cluttered main office to his own large desk at the back. And he found Bob Bannatyne, newly returned from vacation, just taking off his coat.

Bannatyne looked tanned and well-rested.

"Did you hear?" asked Gilbert.

Bannatyne nodded. "I heard," he said. "Congratulations. How's Joe?"

"He took a nasty graze, lost a lot of blood, but he'll be all right."

Bannatyne lifted his briefcase and put it on his desk. "I got something for you," he said.

Bannatyne opened his briefcase and pulled out a bottle of

Glen Fiddich single-malt scotch. "From the duty-free," he said. "You deserve it." Gilbert took the bottle and gazed at it in genuine admiration. "Oh, and there's something else," said Bannatyne. The bearish detective ruffled through some papers in his briefcase and pulled out some paper-clipped documents. "I had some luck with that bank down in Freeport. Made a friend there, Winston Samuels, has a young family, needed some extra cash. I showed him the photos. He recognized Matchett. And get this, he recognized Tom Webb as well." Bannatyne shook his head, grinning widely. "These are transfer statements." Gilbert glanced them over. "Monies payable from Latham's numbered corporation to the Scuba-Tex account in Freeport. Any idea how Latham fits into all this?"

Gilbert glanced over the amounts on the transfer statements, each in the thousands. "Not yet," he said. "But Alvin's going to deal with us. The Crown's arranging things as we speak. They're going to let me have first go at him. They think that might yield the best result."

"With his lawyer?"

"I haven't got all the details, but as far as I know his lawyer will be behind the glass. He can stop the interview whenever he feels Alvin starts to incriminate himself in anything not covered by the deal."

"What's the Crown willing to offer?"

"I've just got the draft proposal. For Cheryl, it's manslaughter. Any defense lawyer would be able to argue manslaughter, considering the manner of death. The chest wound is indignity to a corpse. That's going to be dropped. The kidnapping and forcible confinement, he took a plea to six years, contingent on the quality of his testimony. Embezzlement charges will be dropped. Attempted murder of a police officer, he took another plea, this one for twelve."

"Is Joe happy with that?"

"Joe would like to see Webb get nailed, so I guess he's all right." Gilbert tapped the transfer statements. "This is going to help a lot. Solomon Sing might want you to take the stand so you can tell everybody about Winston Samuels."

"Who the hell is Solomon Sing?"

"He's with the financial crimes section of the O.P.P." Gilbert shrugged wistfully. "Alvin's old unit."

Bannatyne lapsed into silence. Outside on College Street, traffic moved sluggishly through the grey day.

"Barry, I'm sorry," said Bannatyne. "I'm sorry it had to be Alvin."

"Don't be," said Gilbert. "He's not the same man anymore."

"Has he said anything about Donna Varley?"

"We've got strong circumstantial evidence, Bob, but nothing that directly incriminates him. He's not saying a word."

"Shit."

"Don't worry. If you add the manslaughter to the other two, you're still looking at twenty-five years."

"Which means twelve, if he's a good boy. That's cold comfort."

Gilbert shrugged. "I know you'll keep digging," he said. "I know you'll stick him with Donna Varley sooner or later."

Bannatyne gave him a gruff determined look. "You're damn right I will."

Carol Reid came down the aisle with the morning edition of the *Toronto Star*.

"Did you see this?" she said.

She handed the paper to Gilbert.

Gilbert read the headlines. "Shit," he said. "I don't believe it."

Another story by Ronald Roffey.

"What's it say?" asked Bannatyne.

" 'Veteran Detective asked to resign in wake of Latham

arrest fiasco.' " He looked up from the paper, trying to get used to the news. "I guess we might as well say good-bye to Marsh," he said, taking absolutely no pleasure in this small but personal vindication.

The interview took place the following Friday, Friday the 13th, as it turned out, in the interrogation room of the Homicide Office. Matchett sat across from Gilbert in a loose blue detention center uniform, a cigarette smoldering in the ashtray to his left, a cup of coffee steaming at his right hand. Just like old times. The Carlton Grill, on patrol, sitting across from each other, shooting the shit. Only there was a one-way mirror, and Gilbert knew that behind the window sat the Crown prosecutor, Matchett's defense lawyer, Detective Solomon Sing, and Joe Lombardo.

"The money thing started long before Tom hired Cheryl," he said. "When the Tories were last in power. When was it, seven years ago? And Tom was minister of transportation. He regularly took kickbacks whenever there was any tender, even though the tenders were open to public scrutiny. Go up to Downsview, the MTO building there, you can see how it works. If you're going to pull off a kickback in that kind of risky environment, you have to establish a chain of corruption. I helped Tom establish that chain. They were more or less just straight bribes. Cheryl wasn't in on it then, but she figured out what we were doing. Sure her stepdad was a cabinet minister, but he didn't earn enough to keep a catamaran and a million-dollar home on Grand Bahama Island. You get the Freeport connection now, don't you?"

Matchett talked in a monotone; there was none of the liveliness Gilbert remembered from their patrol days. It was as if Matchett spoke to a stranger, not to the man he had shared a radio car with for seven years during the most pivotal years of their lives. His scalp was now covered with brown stubble;

he looked like a Marine recruit. This was the man who had asked him to get down on his knees and beg for his life last week. Yet there was nothing of that now. This wasn't Matchett seeking payback. This was Matchett the manipulator, trying to get the best deal he could from the Crown. Gilbert felt a deep hollowness inside.

"You live in the same house with Webb, and a woman as smart as Cheryl is bound to see things. Or maybe Dorothy knew and Dorothy told her. I was a little nervous about it at first, I told Tom maybe we ought to do something about Cheryl, I wasn't sure if we could trust her, but Tom told me not to worry. Cheryl never mentioned it. Like she didn't want to know about it. Like it was our business, and she couldn't care less. So I started to relax. They were cash bribes, small bills, we really had nothing to worry about. Tom bought Cheryl things, a car, a horse, some jewelry, and she seemed happy about it. Things were going well. I took my cut. After Dennison, I felt I was owed." He shook his head and a flicker of emotion appeared on his face. "You know what that did to me, Barry?"

"I think I do, Alvin."

Matchett shook his head slowly, meditatively. "All I ever wanted was to be a cop. I should have fought harder. But I didn't want to turn it into . . ." He shrugged. "You know." He looked at the blank wall, turning his head quickly. "I didn't want to bring dishonor to the force. Christ, we were both so young. So I went, and it was like walking into purgatory. It was easy to justify a lot of things after that. Taking kickbacks, figuring things out for Tom, working the tenders like a card shark. I was good, I knew what to do, I knew how to ride the risks, it was my way of getting even."

Gilbert grinned; grinned the way he used to grin sometimes when he and Matchett were in patrol. "So you couldn't have cared less about the money?" he said.

Gilbert expected Matchett to crack a smile but his face remained impassive. "I liked the money," he said. "I liked it a lot. It made me feel free. It made me feel as if I was getting what I deserved." He shook his head. "All you dicks, slaving away for fifty grand a year, I thought that was so funny. I still do. I was rolling in it. Tom was the best thing that ever happened to me."

"Do you think so?"

Matchett's face settled. Was that remorse he saw in his old partner's eyes? "No," he said. He lifted his cigarette and took a long pull. "No, maybe not. He can be such a sanctimonious son-of-a-bitch. But I won't get into that."

The bitterness in Matchett's voice settled like a grey fog. They were silent for nearly a minute. Then Gilbert grew conscious of the silent and unseen rolling of the videotape.

"So when did Cheryl come into it?"

Matchett blew a smokering, stuck his finger through it—an old habit from patrol—and gave Gilbert a vague nod, as if he were growing fatigued by the whole discussion.

"Officially, she was hired in June. But she came to us in March. She was prepared. She had every angle covered. And she was diplomatic. She could have given us an ultimatum; she knew about the kickbacks. But she took the time to persuade us. The whole thing was her idea right from the start. In June, neither Tom nor I knew anything about Larry or Donna, nothing about the blackmail. Her scheme was simple. Embezzle election funds by purportedly hiring the services of her ex-husband's numbered corporation. She worked for him part-time. She had a lot of banking privileges. She arranged a subsidiary account for Scuba-Tex in Freeport. That was going to be convenient for Tom because he had a place down there, and it was offshore enough, at least for our purposes."

"So she more or less used Latham's corporation as a front

for funneling funds to the Bahamas. And Latham didn't know anything about it."

"Latham has his head in the clouds. The guy's a first-class dip-shit. The corporation was really a leftover from one of his father's holdings. He had no interest in it whatsoever. He was more than happy to let Cheryl have the reins. He just wanted to spend all his time at his drafting table or in his garden. If you go into the accounts, which I'm sure you will, you'll see all these checks drawn from the campaign account in Cheryl's handwriting, all made out to Ontario Corporation 601847, all signed by Tom. You trail it to the corporation account, you'll find a bundle of checks payable to Scuba-Tex, Freeport, which on the surface makes perfect sense, because on paper it's the sister franchise to Scuba-Tex, Toronto, and nothing could be more kosher than 601847 paying funds into the Scuba-Tex account. At the front end, the campaign account has receipts from 601847, so that the amounts we embezzled all look like legitimate expenses. It was a great scheme. I told you Cheryl was smart. She structured the Freeport account so we all had signing privileges. None of us could withdraw more than five thousand at a time. The bank gave notification whenever money was withdrawn. That more or less protected us from each other. She had all the fail-safes in place. And she was a dynamo as a fund-raiser. But then she said she wanted fifty thousand. She was acting strange. We knew something was going on. Tom asked me to work something out. She was scared. It didn't take me long. I think she wanted to tell someone. By this time we were . . . you know . . . and Jane was getting to be a pain, sniffing around . . . and I think Cheryl really wanted to tell someone, about Paul Varley, about the blackmail, and because we were . . . you know, intimate, I think she thought I could protect her. So she told me about the twenty-five grand each to Larry and

Donna, and I got nervous because she was all mixed up. Ever since Paul Varley, she hasn't really seen things straight, was so loaded up with guilt . . ." For the first time Matchett looked Gilbert right in the eyes. "Honest, Barry, she was pathetic. I felt really sorry for her. I thought if I could straighten her out . . . running from that dead man in the snow for twenty-five years, and I don't know why she felt guilty because he beat her black and blue. But that's Cheryl. Tortured by her conscience. Thinking if she could just order her life well enough, her problems would go away. So I gave her a good shake. I mean I really shook her. I wanted her to pay attention. I shook her so hard she had bruises on her arms. And I told her that if she thought Donna and Larry would stop at the twenty-five apiece she was crazy. This was chronic. I could see that. You remember that blackmail thing we had on patrol, the guy in the bakery, and that woman, that real low-life—it was like that. Donna and Larry, real low-lifes. They weren't going to stop. A couple of leeches like that? Forget it."

Matchett took a final drag on his cigarette and stubbed it out.

"So you offered them three thousand each and gave them a warning," said Gilbert.

Matchett stared at Gilbert hard, taken off guard by this remark. But then he smiled, admiring his old partner's tradecraft.

"I see you've done your homework."

"You gave them a warning, and Larry took the warning, but Donna didn't, Donna decided she was going to try again, and that's when you killed Donna."

Matchett lifted a finger warningly. "You know, Goodhaven's going to come through that door in three seconds flat if you keep this up. I'm holding up my end of it, Barry. I mention Donna in passing. I'll just say this: we weren't going to stand for any impediments. *I* wasn't going to stand for any impediments. I misjudged. I thought I fixed the problem. I thought with Donna and Larry . . . I thought Cheryl would bury old ghosts, but she didn't. She got scared. She collected documents. She hid them. She thought those documents would protect her. When I told Tom . . . he was just too busy to know about it, he was introducing the cutback legislation in the House the next day, he just said deal with it, like it was my problem, like he didn't have his hands in the pie. Fuck him. I think he thought I was some kind of janitor. It was my job to clean up. He didn't care how I did it. And Jane was pissing me off. She was snooping. I found her on two different occasions going through the accounts. So that was something else I had to deal with. I had Cheryl in a powder-keg condition, on the verge of a nervous breakdown, threatening me with sensitive bank statements. I had Jane Ireland digging deeper and deeper, just hoping for a chance to crucify me. And it was like Tom Webb didn't even know me anymore, setting me up to take the fall if Cheryl finally caved. I didn't like going over to Cheryl's, she got that bird a week before Christmas, and she would joke about it in her nervous little way, called it her guard-bird, but I really hated the thing."

He leaned back in his chair and folded his hands on top of his head. Gilbert waited.

"I really thought of it as a game after a while," said Matchett. "Risk management, that's what we call it at work, and I enjoyed the game because it was going to pit me against the same people who had ruined my life, the police. And it also gave me the opportunity to show them—to show you—in a backhanded way, that I was still a good cop, that I could play the evidence game, the investigative game, just as well as you could. My risks were Cheryl, Tom, and Jane. And the more

I thought about it, the more I realized I could have that quarter million free and clear. All I had to do was neutralize my risks."

"You've got manslaughter on Cheryl," said Gilbert. "You might as well tell me. I know you want to."

He took a deep breath, grew solemn, lifted his lighter between his thumb and middle finger and turned it end on end a few times on the table. "I knew you would see the tire tracks in the snow. My first problem was a car. My own car was out of the question. A stolen car? No, too many risks. A rented car. Maybe. But that left a paper trail. Then I thought, get Jane to bring the car. In fact, build a line of evidence that leads to Jane. The Sorels, the bullet, the hair. I thought if I could arrange it so Jane took the fall, she would be out of the way. At the very least, it would buy some time."

"So you had Webb leave a message on her voice mail asking her to bring a car from the pool?"

A grin came to Matchett's face. "Before we had voice mail, we had answering machines. When we got voice mail, we got rid of all our answering machines. There were a lot of old message tapes around. I checked them all. I found an old message, Webb asking Jane to bring a car to Mount Joseph. I guess this was from when Dorothy was dying. Jane went out for coffee and I rigged the message onto her voice mail." Matchett's grin broadened. "I was really pleased when I came up with this idea. It gave me an additional decoy, Webb's voice on Jane's voice mail, a way to at least implicate him as an accomplice in Cheryl's murder. He was setting me up, and I wanted to provide myself with some protection. He didn't know anything about the car, but let's remember, he told me to do something about Cheryl. So in that sense he really is an accomplice. He wanted her out of the way, but he wanted plausible deniability as well. I knew how the game was played. It gave me a great sense of satisfaction to manipulate all this false evidence so intricately. The ultimate purpose was of course to throw you off completely, but there was part of me that wanted to show you how good I was. I wanted my handiwork admired."

"So you got in the car and you drove to the Glenarden."

Matchett frowned. "You're missing the point, Barry. It was all very carefully planned. I knew about the security monitor in the lobby of the Glenarden. I had to wait for a cold day, a day when I could legitimately be bundled up, so that when you scrutinized the tape, as I knew you would, you would just see a man in a parka with his head in his hood, and his face covered with a balaclava. Typical winter gear for such a cold day. I just didn't pick any day." He took a deep breath and brought his hands down from his head and put them back on the table. "Then there was the problem of how to get her down to the car without a lot of noise. She let me in. I said I just wanted to talk to her. She was still in her exercise stuff. I went up there and fixed some drinks. I told her we might have some legal difficulties. Before I knew it, she was on the phone to Latham, asking about a lawyer. I cut the call short. I said I was hungry, so she went into the kitchen to get some food, and while she was in the kitchen, I put the Kedamine into her drink. Strong stuff. She had about two sips, and she started to feel woozy, and I think she guessed what was going on. She panicked. She got up and backed away from me and that's when she let that damn bird out of the cage. You have to admire her. I went crazy. I was so completely distracted by that parrot being loose in the room she was able get to the bathroom with the portable phone. I got control of myself and just let the bird fly. I ran to the bathroom, grabbed her by the hair, and smashed her head against the mirror. I think she dropped the phone, I can't remember, all I heard was that bird squawking out in the living room. Cheryl looked at me for a second or two, then she just slumped. I pulled her out into the hall. I thought all her neighbors must have heard the commotion."

Matchett looked pale, and a film of perspiration had appeared on his head.

"I just tried to kill all my nerve endings at that point," he said. "I still had a lot to do, I had to search her apartment, then go up to her work and search there. So I went back out into the living room and I saw the parrot perched on the curtain rod. It didn't fly away from me. It just stared at me, turning its head this way and that, trying to figure out what I was going to do. Even when I was just a few feet away, it just stared at me. I guess they're used to humans. I grabbed it and I choked it. It took a few minutes, but I finally killed it. Then I just stood there and got a grip on myself. I cleaned up the glasses and put them away. I generally tidied up. Then I walked back into the hall and saw that Cheryl had moved herself back into the bathroom."

"She was in there covering the phone with toilet paper," said Gilbert. "She was already trying to leave clues."

Matchett shrugged. "I guess so. And I guess I missed the phone. I was more concerned about just getting her out of there. If someone suddenly showed up at the door..." Matchett lifted his pack of DuMauriers and stared at the cancer warning. "I had to get her out. So I rolled her up in the carpet. I took her to the laundry room and pushed her out the window. Then I climbed out the window myself. I wanted to avoid the lobby monitor. I took her out of the carpet and put her into the trunk. I had no idea she was going to freeze to death. I wasn't even thinking about that. I brought the carpet upstairs. It was late. There was no one in the halls. I put the carpet back down and began my search. I knew I should have gotten rid of the parrot but I couldn't bring myself to touch it. And what was I going to do with it anyway? I could leave it there, that was a clue, or I could take it away, that was a clue as well; either way, it was evidence, so I decided to leave it. I couldn't find the documents. I didn't even think of going near the cage. The cage was just a blank spot in the room. So I left the apartment and I went up to the CNIB. How long does it take a person to freeze to death in that kind of weather? By that time, she'd been in the trunk an hour. I checked her office, no documents. I got mad. I knew then I had to kill her. In fact I knew I was going to have to kill her . . . well, a day or two after she found out Donna had been murdered."

"So really we're talking premeditated murder," said Gilbert.

Matchett glanced over his shoulder at the one-way glass. "I don't think Goodhaven likes to hear things like that."

"You've got your deal, the manslaughter charge, what difference does it make?"

"As long as we understand each other."

"Just go ahead," said Gilbert. "You're starting to get on my nerves."

Matchett pulled a cigarette from his pack and lit up. "There's not much more to say. Choice of gun. Why would I use my own gun? Why not buy a gun from any of the peddlers on Church, on Jarvis, unregistered, untraced, thrown away after the murder? Again, because I needed something solid for Jane. I really enjoyed that, pretending I was trying to protect Jane when you kept asking about the key. I really had you going."

"Alvin, I never bought it. It smelled fixed right from the start to me."

The smile faded from Matchett's face and he looked disgruntled. "Yeah . . . well . . . at least Marsh fucked up. I never liked him. Even way back when."

"Marsh is a good cop."

"Marsh is an asshole."

"Let's stick to the subject," said Gilbert. "You drove her down to Cherry Beach, a nice deserted spot . . ."

Matchett nodded, his eyes narrowing, took a long

contemplative drag on his cigarette then let the smoke drift out in two thin columns from his nose. "What we used to call a dump job," he said. He looked at Gilbert. "Remember? A dump job. The hardest thing in the world to solve because the victim has no relation to their surroundings, there's nowhere for the detective to start. I open the trunk and she's not moving. She's not breathing. And her skin's gone this grey color. I touch her wrist. Cold. I think to myself, holy fuck, she's frozen. So I lift her out, and I'm so startled by the way she feels that I lose my grip and she falls in the snow. She's kind of stiff, not inordinately so, but I knew she had to be dead. I lift her up again and I carry her out to the beach and drop her there. And I was just going to leave. But then I thought about Laraby. I knew she was dead but what if . . . what if I drive away and she somehow miraculously gets up the way Laraby did, and walks to the nearest police station and reports me. Plus I had to leave a bullet for Jane's sake. So I shot her. And I was going to drive away, but then I saw a car coming down Cherry Street, and I didn't want to be caught red-handed, so I loaded her back into the trunk, and headed back. Then the car pulls a U-turn at the bridge. I think to myself, I don't want this body in the trunk. I've got to get it out. So I take the next turn off, the Dominion Malting pier, and I dump her there. Finished. Done. The perfect crime. All I had to do was wait for Tom and Jane to fall like dominoes."

Matchett gave him a self-deprecating shrug. And Gilbert had to admit to himself, there was a certain ingenuity about the whole thing. But just as an investigator often lost control of his investigation, it seemed a perpetrator nearly always lost control of his crime. Matchett looked at him, and Gilbert didn't know what he was expecting, but he was certainly expecting something.

"It was the grease, wasn't it?" said Matchett. "The grease on the parka."

Gilbert nodded.

Matchett continued, critiquing his own crime. "The rest of it was pretty much circumstantial. The Kedamine, sure I burgled the animal clinic but that didn't necessarily tie me to Cheryl. The missing gun. I've already explained that. The money, Larry Varley, my affair with Cheryl, none of it was conclusive. It was the grease. And the paint chips under the rug. You matched the paint chips to the laundry room window, you matched the grease, and you had my parka."

Gilbert nodded. "One after the other," he said. "Like dominoes."

"You can see why I decided to cooperate."

"Actually, the grease wasn't your biggest mistake."

Matchett's eyes widened. "It wasn't?"

"The car was."

Matchett now looked truly puzzled. "I don't get it."

Gilbert leaned forward to explain. "All we got from the crime scene was Michelin XGTs. Tire marks. We did some checking. At least twelve different makes and models come with Michelin XGTs. Then you have to take into consideration all the Michelin XGTs used as replacement tires. Your big mistake was when you tried to run me down on Prestine Heights Boulevard. That gave us a good make on the car, the midnight blue Crown Victoria. Maybe it wasn't even the same Crown Victoria you used for Cheryl, but there's seven in the pool, and it got us looking in that direction."

Matchett was more perplexed than ever. "But I never tried to run you down, Barry," he said. His brow furrowed in utter and genuine mystification. "You think after all my careful planning I'd be stupid enough to try and run you down?"

To Gilbert, the room suddenly felt a lot warmer. "Then if you didn't try to run me down," he said, "who did?"

Chapter Twenty

Solomon Sing arrested the Honorable Thomas Webb, member for Sudbury West, the following Monday afternoon while the legislature was in session. Not only did it make headlines in Ontario, but across the country. Gilbert lay in bed next to Regina watching the coverage on Global TV. He shook his head to himself. He wasn't sure how he felt about this. Sometimes a murder investigation could get away from you. Ronald Roffey had already phoned him twice, as had a half dozen other reporters. So far, he hadn't returned any of their calls.

He watched as the regular legislative cameras caught Detective Solomon Sing and two uniformed officers of the Ontario Provincial Police enter the red-carpeted Assembly Chamber and present the arrest warrant to Webb. Webb, a prominent front-bencher, sat in the chair next to Premier Willis. Premier Willis' face went blank as Solomon Sing, a tall austere man of Malaysian origin, began to read from the warrant.

"I don't know if I can watch this," he said. "This is so pathetic. How many times are they going to show it?"

Regina grinned as she marked some grade eleven test-papers. "I like Sing," she said. "He's so unflappable."

Webb stood up, an unmistakable figure in the Chamber, with his mane of white hair, and addressed the Speaker, as if it were the Speaker's concern. How many times would they hear it? Mr. Speaker, this is an outrage. Please have the Sergeant-at-Arms eject these . . . and now Premier Willis stood up, put his hands on Webb's shoulder, asked him to sit down, struggled to spare his government as much embarrassment as possible. The scene cut to the north entrance of the Parliament Buildings, where Webb, looking shell-shocked, his hands cuffed behind his back, was escorted to a waiting unmarked car by Detective Sing and the two O.P.P. officers. The segment ended and the scene cut to Raiva Bhupal, Global's Queen's Park reporter, who could only say that the chairman of the Management Board had been arrested on numerous corruption charges and that the allegations connecting him to the murder of Cheryl Latham had been neither confirmed nor denied by investigators.

Gilbert flicked off the television. He felt uncomfortable. Regina put her hand on his arm. He looked up at her. She was the one beautiful constant in his life. "I don't know," he said. "Did you see the look in his eyes when they brought him down the steps? I just wrecked that man's life. He's never going to be the same again."

She gave him a pat. "You didn't wreck it, Barry," she said. "He did."

Susan Allen, Wesley Rowe's social worker at Mount Joseph Hospital, lived in Willowdale, one of the more settled and affluent suburbs, on a quiet street of thirty-year-old split-levels and ranch styles. Susan Allen's husband, the same man Gilbert had seen a few weeks ago in Susan Allen's office, stood at the foot of the stairs reading the search warrant while Lombardo and two officers began going through the house, looking for the typewriter. Derek Allen had grown a mustache, an effete line of bristles, and kept stroking either side of it as Gilbert stood there waiting. All the furniture in the living room was covered with plastic; it looked more like a protected museum display than a living room.

The house was a split-level. A half-flight of stairs led to the upstairs, another half-flight down to a large den with sliding glass doors, a bathroom, and door leading to the two-car garage.

"Is the garage down there?" said Gilbert. The question was more a polite indication that he now wished to search the garage.

Allen looked up with mild trepidation. "You want to go in the garage?"

Gilbert gave him a friendly shrug. "Might as well check it?" he said.

Allen now stared at him. Already unsettled by their arrival, he now looked downright nervous. "But you're looking for her typewriter," he said. "It wouldn't be in the garage."

"Why don't you tell us where it is then?" said Gilbert.

At first he couldn't answer. But then he said, "I don't really live here. I . . ."

Gilbert gave him an understanding nod. "Okay," he said, "then I'll . . ." He headed down the stairs. "If you don't mind. Just to make things go quicker. I hate to disturb you on your lunch hour like this."

Allen took an apprehensive step after him. "But I really don't think . . ."

Gilbert open the garage door. Two ten-speeds hung on an overhead rack, a workbench stood against the wall, and a car with a big plastic cover over it stood parked in the middle.

He stared at the car. Because he recognized the car. And he felt his shoulders sinking. It looked as if it hadn't been driven in a long time. It looked as if it had been hidden here on purpose. A midnight blue Crown Victoria. He heard Allen come down to the doorway. Gilbert glanced over his shoulder and the two men stared at each other. He knew that Allen understood. There was nothing that could be done now. He walked to the front of the car and lifted the plastic cover. He knelt by the fender. She hadn't even bothered to clean it. In the mud on the fender he saw a clear impression of the weave of his own pants. He looked over his shoulder at Allen.

"Is this your wife's car?" he asked.

"Yes," said Allen. "Yes, it is."

Allen continued to stare; he looked like the kind of man who might have had a serious drinking problem at one time but now had gotten over it. He gave Gilbert a barely perceptible nod.

"I think I better call her," he said. He turned to go.

Did Allen realize with that one simple statement, more or less an admission to his collusion, he himself was now facing charges? That he knew about Susan's attempted murder of a police officer but failed to report it? He stood up and sighed. Marsh's life, destroyed. Webb's life, destroyed. And now the Allens. And what about Matchett? Would he find it funny that the most important clue in breaking the Latham case turned out to be this Crown Victoria, a car that had absolutely nothing to do with Cheryl's murder? He stood up, put his hands on his hips, and stared at the car, fighting against his old pervasive cynicism, trying to recognize the irony of the situation. He could take that only so far. Marsh and the Allens were good people who had made human mistakes. And because Barry Gilbert had been added to the equation, they were going to pay a heavy price. Both Susan and Marsh had simply been trying to protect their jobs, jobs put on the line by Webb's spending cuts. Yet vehicular manslaughter seemed extreme, and he couldn't help wondering what Susan Allen must have been thinking as she stepped on the accelerator, whether she had been in her right mind or if she had had a momentary lapse, whether murder was her intent or if, coming to Parkview Hills to talk to Gilbert, she had simply lost control of herself in a blinding fit of rage. He would have to ask the Crown Attorney about her defense strategy if and when she went to trial.

Lombardo appeared at the door, his hair now short because of his head wound treatment. He looked good; Lombardo could go bald and still look good. He held a Smith-Corona cartridge typewriter in his hands.

"We found it," he said.

Gilbert glanced back at Lombardo, trying to hide the cold wind that he felt blowing through his body.

"Yeah," he said. He gestured at the car. "So did I."

The auditorium was packed with police officers, detectives, their wives, and families. Deputy Chief Ling, a precise Chinese man, a second generation Canadian whose parents had come from Hong Kong in the thirties, stood at the front in full uniform. Sign of the times, thought Gilbert, sitting near the back by himself, the MTPFs first non-Anglo Deputy Chief of Detective Support Command, and a damn fine one. Ling spoke into the microphone.

"Detective Giovanni Lombardo," he said.

Lombardo, in a new suit, climbed the steps to the platform.

"For honor and courage in the abduction of murder suspect Alvin James Matchett, you are hereby awarded the Detective Award," said Ling.

Gilbert couldn't help thinking of Matchett's award, the one he never got, the one for saving Patrol Officer Barry Gilbert's life, the one for finally stopping the crazed Laraby all those many years ago. At least Joe was a getting an award.

Lombardo took the plaque, a well-respected and coveted award, and shook Ling's hand. Then he saluted crisply and marched off the stage. Half the women in the audience just about fainted. Gilbert couldn't help grinning. He had mixed feelings about the ceremonial trappings of a paramilitary organization like the MTPF, but today his feelings were nothing but positive. Lombardo left the stage to cheers and loud applause. A month ago, Joe was on Marsh's preliminary discharge and layoff list. Now he had the Detective Award. What a difference a decent collar could make in a detective's career.

Lombardo walked up the aisle while Ling called upon the next recipient. Gilbert got up and gave him a gruff shake of the hand.

"Congratulations," he said. "I thought I might buy you a drink."

"Actually, I've got someone waiting for me," he said.

This didn't surprise Gilbert; Joe always bounced back fast.

"Oh, yeah?" said Gilbert. "Do I know her?"

"Yeah," said Lombardo, "you do. You might as well say hello. She's right up here. I was afraid she wasn't going to make it. She said she had to work late. But I saw her sneak in at the last minute."

They walked together toward the back of the auditorium. And Gilbert saw her. A tall, beautiful mulatto woman. Sonia Bailey. Cheryl's next door neighbor from the Glenarden.

She gave him a smile, a shrug, and a wave. Maybe something good was going to come out of this after all. He waved back, then stopped.

"Actually, you two go ahead," he said. "I think I'm going to stay for the rest of the ceremony. I want to see McGuire get his citation, that guy from Bomb Squad who lost his hand."

"Are you sure?"

Gilbert nodded. "Go ahead," said Gilbert. He glanced at Sonia. "I can see she loves short guys."

But he didn't stay for the rest of the ceremony. He took the College streetcar over to Sherbourne Street and walked up to the Carlton Grill, the restaurant he and Matchett always used to go to back when they were both in patrol, didn't know why, just felt he had to, hadn't been there in years, had to look at it once more, had to somehow convince himself that the seven years he had spent with Matchett in patrol had indeed been good years, possibly the best years, years that would always occupy a golden spot in his memory. Sherbourne Street, where street drunks and panhandlers ruled. A place of rooming houses, cheap hotels, and even cheaper bars. He entered the Carlton Grill. Came here first in the late sixties, when he had been a student at architectural school. And it hadn't changed much. Big fast food kitchen in the middle, with huge overhead vents, a counter all the way around, and tables against the walls. A vintage diner. A classic diner. Somehow appealing in its crass ugliness.

He walked past the kitchen, glancing around to see if he knew any of the cooks, any of the waiters, but he recognized none. The 1970s now seemed a long time ago. Didn't recognize anybody, and yet the place was full of ghosts. He could see these ghosts, people who were now probably long dead. There was George, cracking eggs with one hand over the grill, flipping bacon with the other, cigarette hanging from his mouth, expertly blowing the ash upward, where it was carried away by the overhead vent. And there was Bonnie, in her pink uniform and apron, hip thrust to the left, order pad ready, gazing at her next customer as if she sincerely suspected the level of his or her intelligence. And there was Hank, the linen service truck driver, who always stopped in for an egg sandwich and a coffee at this time of the day, as skinny as a starved rooster, in his workman's blues, never saying anything to anybody, just staring, as if somehow the antics at the Carlton Grill bewildered him.

He found the table at the front, second from the end, their old table, and sat down; they hadn't changed the furniture in forty years. The waiter came by and he ordered a coffee and brown toast, his old standby. He stared at the empty chair across from him. And he saw ghosts again. Matchett was sitting in that chair. Matchett was having his cigarette and coffee. Only it was a much younger Matchett. A Matchett who hadn't been corrupted by his own bitterness. A Matchett who still believed in something. The waiter came with his coffee and toast. George kept breaking eggs at the grill, a ghost, hovering around the present-day short-order cook. Was it really so long ago? Was he really forty-eight years old, with a wife and two teenaged daughters?

He took a sip of coffee. He wasn't an architect but he still felt as if he had made something worthwhile of his life. Life was precious. You had to step back and watch it every so often, just so you could appreciate every minute. He felt wistful as he again thought of Matchett. Matchett would be in his sixties by the time he got out of prison. There wouldn't be much of life left for Matchett when he got out.

His pager beeped, and he looked down at the digital display. He turned the beeper off; he didn't readily recognize the phone number. He got up, went to the public telephone in the foyer, and dialed the number.

John Levinson, the Crown prosecutor in the Wesley Rowe case, answered the phone.

"I knew you were anxious about this," said the lawyer, "so I had my secretary page you. We're going to drop the charges in the Wesley Rowe case. The match on the typewriter helped us but we were already leaning that way anyway. He's not mentally competent to stand trial. Nor was he competent to look after his mother. We can't reasonably hold him accountable for his actions. The papers are on their way to the Don Jail. He should be released tomorrow. I've already let Judith Wendeborn know."

"Thanks, John."

"Don't thank me, Barry. If I had more staff around here he never would have been arraigned in the first place." There was a pause as Gilbert heard the shuffling of papers on the other end of the line. "Oh, and I talked to Claude Rice. About the Susan Allen case? Ironic, but she's going to plead incompetence too. She has no recollection of the night she tried to run you down. The same thing happened when she was seventeen. She lit a friend's house on fire, had no recollection of it. The lawyer in that case presented a stack of psychiatric reports, so there's a history, here, Barry, and the judge will probably just order evaluation and treatment. Is that okay with you?"

Gilbert thought of Susan Allen's Crown Victoria, how without it they never would have nailed Alvin; how, without it, they never would have gotten their embezzlement and conspiracy to commit murder charges against the Honorable Thomas Webb.

"Whatever the judge wants is fine by me," he said.

He went back to his table and finished his coffee. Two boosts in one day. Lombardo gets the Detective Award, and the charges in the Wesley Rowe case are dismissed. The past was sometimes golden, but the present wasn't so bad either, he decided. He took one last bite of toast and slid a couple of toonies on the table. That should cover it, and give the waiter a decent tip besides. He left the grill and walked out into the pleasant April afternoon. He crossed the street—he wanted to walk on the sunny side. Sunshine all around, but with snow clouds on the horizon, moving in from Mississauga, getting closer. The weatherman was calling for fifteen centimeters. April in Toronto, and winter was reluctant to ease its tenacious grip.

As he reached the far sidewalk he turned around and took one last look at the Carlton Grill. A patrol car drove up, parked in front, and two young officers—neither could be more than thirty—got out, laughing, talking, heading into the grill, conspicuous in their uniforms, feeling special because of their uniforms, in the best days of their lives. They strutted. They exuded energy. They were vibrant. That was him, twenty years ago. That was him and Matchett going into the Carlton Grill.

He turned away and walked north on Sherbourne, up past the Wellesley Hospital and the Our Lady of Lourdes Catholic Church. He turned left on Isabella past the old Isabella Hotel, where even this early in the day the prostitutes were hanging around street corners, in impossibly short dresses and three-inch heels. He headed toward Jarvis Street. Toward the old building. All the old ghosts were pushing him along. He turned right at Jarvis Street and headed north. And he decided he really did miss all the bright young students drifting up and down the street from Jarvis Collegiate Institute. He missed the panhandlers and the drunks. And despite his many running battles in patrol with the Isabella Street hookers, he even missed them, now felt a fond regard for them. It always baffled him, why they chose Isabella, two blocks away from his old headquarters.

He crossed the street and stood in front of the old police building. Built in 1953, six storeys tall, red brick, like a giant wedding cake, with neat rows of small windows. A building full of memories. A building full of ghosts. The Catholic Children's Aid Society was in there now. So was the Congress of

Black Women. The white paint around the windows was now peeling badly; in fact, the entire building looked as if it had been let go. Yet in Gilbert's memory it glowed. He thought of the new building. And then he thought of this old building. And he knew he had to move forward. He had to move forward, even if he had to pull the weight of the past behind him, the way the little boy pulled the immense obelisk in his toy wagon. He knew he could accept it now, that his memories of Matchett were still golden, that they would always stay golden, and that recent events didn't in any way cheapen them. Matchett was just a man. And his life was a river. You went along with the flow and sometimes the scenery was pleasant. Sometimes it wasn't. You had to make the most of where the river took you.

He turned from the old building and walked toward Yonge Street. For now, he would enjoy the sunshine. The warmth on his face was refreshing after the long Toronto winter. He glanced up at the snow clouds. He would enjoy the sunshine until the snow finally came again.